Contemporary Philosophy of Religion

𝓗𝓔𝓑 ☼ Humanities-Ebooks, LLP

Humanities-Ebooks

Humanities-Ebooks.co.uk publishes academic and educational Ebooks in English, History, Philosophy and related areas.

It has a rapidly expanding list of searchable titles ranging from scholarly texts to student introductions, some of which contain colour illustrations and internal and external hyperlinks not reproducible in printed form.

For the current list please visit

http://www.humanities-ebooks.co.uk

Our titles are also available to Libraries in PDF through Ebrary, EBSCO and Ingram.

Contemporary Philosophy of Religion

Steven M. Duncan

𝓗𝓔𝓑 ✭ Humanities-Ebooks, LLP

© Steven Duncan, 2007, 2009

The Author has asserted his right to be identified as the author of this Work in accordance with the Copyright, Designs and Patents Act 1988.

Published electronically in 2007 by *Humanities-Ebooks.co.uk*
Tirril Hall, Tirril, Penrith CA10 2JE

This paperback version published in 2009.

ISBN 978-1-84760-053-0 EBOOK
ISBN 978-1-84760-096-7 PAPERBACK

Contents

What is the Philosophy of Religion?	7
Three Competing Paradigms in Contemporary Philosophy of Religion	10
Deductivism	13
Neo-Thomism	14
Analytic Philosophy	16
Analytic Atheism and the Meaningfulness of Religious Language	18
Atheistic Deductivism	23
Inductivism	27
Mitchell's Inductivist Proposal	29
Swinburne's Bayesian Theism	30
Swinburne on the Prior Probability of Theism	33
Swinburne's Positive Case for Theism	35
Swinburne's Theodicy	41
Inference to the Best Explanation and the Future of Inductivism	45
Post-Deductivism	47
Deductivism and the Ethics of Belief	49
The Post-Deductivists on Evil	51
The Parity Argument Strategy	53
Plantinga's Reformed Epistemology	55
Plantinga and Wolterstorff: Christian Philosophy	58
Recent Work on the Traditional Arguments for God's Existence	61
The Ontological Argument	61
The Cosmological Argument	63
The Teleological Argument	67
Bibliography	71

Chapter One

What is the Philosophy of Religion?

Philosophy as traditionally understood may be defined as the branch of intellectual inquiry that deals with the most general and fundamental questions about the nature of reality and human life insofar as those problems lie beyond the competence of the special sciences to raise or resolve. Defined in this way, many people do not want there be such a thing as philosophy, or at any rate want as little of it as possible.[1] However, despite the concerted efforts of many movements in twentieth century philosophy, from logical positivism to post-modernism, this traditional conception of philosophy has proven remarkably resilient and philosophers continue to discuss the "big questions" with ever less embarrassment as the mid-twentieth century slips farther below the horizon of living memory. Among the questions that have exercised philosophers of the last sixty years, that of the existence of God has been one of the most hotly contested. It is the debate over that question that will be subject of this book.

Philosophy of Religion is the branch of philosophy that deals with that question, as well as related questions concerning the nature of God, the meaning of religious language and the immortality of the soul, among others, insofar as these questions are amenable to discussion from the point of view of neutral, impartial rational inquiry. Unlike other "second-order" philosophical pursuits, however, the philosophy of religion does not take religion as such, i.e. actual religious belief and practice, as its subject-matter. Instead, philosophy of religion is con-

---

1   For example, Quine is supposed to have said that "philosophy of science is philosophy enough;" this, or something like it, expresses the opinion of many contemporary philosophers.

centrated primarily on the metaphysical truth-claims implied or presupposed by religious belief and practice properly so-called and attempts to bring these to the surface, analyze their central concepts, clarify their implications and evaluate their truth or falsity from the rational point of view. Since most religions make some attempt to do this from within the perspective of belief in the form of dogmatic theology, it is religion as theologically articulated, rather than as lived belief and practice, that is primarily of interest to philosophers of religion, regardless of whether or not they are sympathetic to religion.

The religious tradition of the West, which for our purposes here includes the Middle East and Persia, is known as *monotheism*, centrally characterized by the thesis, shared by Christians, Jews and Muslims, that there exists one supreme being, the personal and providential creator of the universe who reveals Himself through the prophets and whose mighty deeds are recorded in canonical scriptures such as the Bible or the Holy Qu'ran. Although these religions differ with regard to which prophets and scriptures they accept and diverge with regard to their distinctive religious teachings, all of them trace themselves to the fundamental revelation of God to Abraham and claim to worship the same God. Furthermore, as theologically articulated, they largely agree in their overall metaphysical conception of God. It is this conception of God, known as *theism*, which is the primary object of analysis in the philosophy of religion and which is thought to express the fundamental metaphysical truth-claims common to all the Western monotheistic faiths.

The theological consensus among monotheists goes deeper than this, however; the mainstream conception of the theistic God, shared by the major figures of all three traditions, is nowadays referred to as Classical Theism or Perfect Being theology.[1] According to this view, God is characterized as the "being a greater than which cannot be conceived", i.e. as the most perfect being in principle, unsurpassable even by Himself. Reflecting to some extent an element of Platonic inheritance, God is thought of as a being so fully and completely realized in every respect as to be immutable, impassable and utterly self-sufficient in such a way as to require nothing outside of Himself in order to exist. At the same time, God is a personal being, possessing intellect and will and thus capa-

---

1 See especially the works of Thomas V. Morris, in particular his *Anselmian Explorations* (1988) and *The Concept of God* (1989).

ble of rational agency. One way in which God has exercised this rational agency is in the creation of the observable universe from nothing pre-existent, whether this is conceived of as eternally existing matter or the very substance of God Himself. Rather, God created the world *ex nihilo* simply through willing that it should exist; further, given that the observable universe is created from nothing, it requires not only to be created but to be *conserved* by God at every moment at which it exists. Thus, despite being wholly independent of and transcendent to the observable universe He has created, God is immanent in presence and power to every point in space and time. In the context of the divine perfection, we must therefore attribute omnipotence, omniscience and perfect goodness to God, which attributes are reflecting in and testified to by what He has made.

In addition, most Classical Theists include necessary existence as among the divine attributes, maintaining that God, being independent and self-sufficient, contains within Himself the cause, reason or explanation for His existence. In the context of the divine perfection, Classical Theists deny that God is subject either to coming-to-be or passing-away. Being incapable of ever having come into existence or of ever going out of existence, God thus possesses infinity and eternity. However, Classical Theists are divided over whether this eternity should be understood as existence for an infinite period of time in both directions or as constituted by a unique, non-temporal mode of existence outside of time. In addition, some modern exponents of necessary existence as one of the central divine attributes maintain that it ought to be understood as *logically necessary* existence and thus as entailing that God's non-existence, properly understood, is logically impossible or self-contradictory. The classical ontological argument for God's existence, to found in Anselm, Descartes and moderns such as Norman Malcolm and Alvin Plantinga, is an expression of this tendency, though not all theistic philosophers, not even all Classical Theists, endorse this idea.[1]

Much work has been done to clarify and defend the Classical Theist conception of God, as well as to evaluate it, especially in comparison to other, alternative conceptions of God on offer in contemporary philosophy of religion. We cannot go into all this here; however, we will focus on the central question of the philosophy of religion, namely, the question of God's existence, from the philosophical point of view. For our purposes here, we may further divide this topic

---

1 For a collection of classic sources, see Plantinga (1965).

into two more specific issues. First, there is the question of whether or not there are any rationally compelling (or at least intellectually respectable) arguments, evidence or grounds for believing that God exists. Theistic philosophers of religion generally defend an affirmative answer to this question, whereas atheistic philosophers of religion critique those defences and conclude that there is no good reason for believing that God exists. Secondly, there is the problem of evil, which examines the main piece of evidence for positive atheism, i.e. the affirmative judgment that there is no God. Since the mid-twentieth century, the problem of evil has been one of the most written on philosophical topics in the English-speaking world. No account of contemporary philosophy of religion can fail to deal with this issue at least in broad outline.

Three Competing Paradigms in Contemporary Philosophy of Religion

I will survey contemporary philosophy of religion in accordance with the historical thesis I advanced in my earlier, more comprehensive treatment of this material called *Analytic Philosophy of Religion: Its History since 1955*.[1] According to that treatment, contemporary philosophy of religion is best characterized as reflecting the interaction between three overlapping but successive paradigms in the philosophy of religion called Deductivism, Inductivism and post-Deductivism respectively. While each of these approaches to the questions of God's existence and problem of evil has adherents today, each also enjoyed a period in which it was the prime focus of attention within the discipline. Deductivism, which was initiated by the neo-Thomists and which drew the fire of the analytic atheists, was dominant in the crucial decade of the 1950's in which contemporary philosophy of religion emerged, emphasized the construction and evaluation of deductive proofs of God's existence, and gave rise to the deductive Argument from Evil intended to prove God's non-existence. In response to theistic critiques of the Argument from Evil, the discussion of God's existence slowly shifted from the evaluation of deductive proofs for God's existence to the question of whether or not God's existence was reasonable to believe on the basis of our total evidence; this initiated the Inductivist paradigm that culminated in Richard Swinburne's Bayesian argument for the existence of God. Although what I call the post-

---

1   Published by Humanities-Ebooks (2007).

Deductivist paradigm emerged about the same time as Inductivism, it did not enjoy its heyday until the 1990's, when Alvin Plantinga proposed his "Reformed Epistemology" as the core of a new kind of "Christian philosophy."

Given the constraints of the *Insights* series, I will only be able to barely summarize the stages and movements that characterize contemporary philosophy of religion, though I hope to do enough to pique the reader's interest in consulting the aforementioned text as well as the many fine books referenced here and listed in the bibliography. We will begin by looking at the historical background of contemporary philosophy of religion and the emergence of the Deductivist paradigm.

Chapter Two

Deductivism

Prior to the emergence of modern analytic philosophy, British and American philosophy was dominated by the tradition of German Idealist thought inspired by Hegel. This school conceived of the ultimate reality as an impersonal, self-developing absolute mind or spirit identical with but not exhausted by the observable universe. Given this conception of things, it is not surprising that thinkers in this school were largely opposed to traditional monotheism and rejected traditional Christianity as anything more than a kind of mythical expression of the truth that finds its full and literal expression only in the categories of Hegelian metaphysics.[1] Although Christianity did manage to find defenders even within the Idealist school, what was then known as philosophy of religion was largely just the project of reinterpreting traditional religious ideas within the framework of Hegelian philosophy, where those ideas ceased to have anything like their traditional significance.

By the turn of the twentieth century, the inevitable reaction against Idealism – and Hegelianism in particular – had begun to set in. Under the broad-based banner of neo-Realism, philosophers in Europe, the United Kingdom and the United States began to urge a return to a less arcane philosophical perspective, one more amenable to common sense. One of the contending new realist positions was the philosophical and theological system known as neo-Thomism; another, which grew out of British neo-Realism, gave rise to what became

---

1 For a summary of this tradition, see Sell (1980) and Blanshard (1974).

known as Analytic philosophy. It is in the confrontation of these two schools that contemporary philosophy of religion and its characteristic problems and issues emerged.

Neo-Thomism

Neo-Thomism was a movement that began in the Catholic Church and remained largely within its confines. Although a Thomistic revival was already well underway by the early decades of the nineteenth century, the movement took its primary inspiration from two events that occurred later in the century. The First Vatican Council (1870–71) is remembered now primarily for its definition of the dogma of papal infallibility; in fact, however, that decree was only part of the realization of its more central aim, which was to re-affirm counter-Reformation Catholic theology in the context of the challenges of the modern world. Decrees were also issued against modernism, rationalism, semi-rationalism and evolutionary naturalism.[1] At the same time, fideism and traditionalism were also condemned and among the positive decrees of the Council was the thesis that God's existence was capable of rational proof independently of the claims of faith. In 1879, Pope Leo XIII issued his first encyclical, *Aeterni Patris*, in which he directed that all Catholic seminaries and universities should base their philosophy and theology curriculum on the teachings of St. Thomas Aquinas (1225–74).[2] This encyclical had the effect of making Aquinas the "official" theologian of the Catholic Church and spawned the neo-Thomist movement that would dominate the Catholic philosophy and theology for the next eighty years.

Although a number of distinguished lay thinkers were associated with this movement, the mainstream of Thomist thought remained within the Scholastic manualist tradition, charged with the production of the textbooks used to train generations of Catholic seminarians and college students. In the English-speaking world, the most widely used of these manuals were those produced early in the twentieth century by Cardinal Mercier, G. H. Joyce, R. P. Phillips and Reginald Garrigou-LaGrange, all of whom were Catholic priests. It was characteristic of all of the Scholastic manualists that they attempted to provide deductive, rationally

---

1   See Denzinger (1954) 435–8 and 442–51.
2   See *Acta Apostolica Sedis* (1879) 97 ff.

compelling proofs for God's existence drawn from non-religious considerations. In particular, the manualists attempted to refurbish the "five ways", i.e. the five proofs offered for God's existence in the *Summa Theologiae*, generally regarded as the definitive statement of Aquinas' theological system. Perhaps the most rigorous of these writers was Garrigou-LaGrange (1883–1964), whose *God: His Existence and Nature*, is a classic explication of the neo-Thomist approach to the question of God's existence.[1]

Garrigou begins by making explicit reference to the teachings of Vatican I, insisting that Catholic doctrine demands that God's existence be capable of rigorous, certainty-conferring rational demonstration from self-evident first principles. Like Thomas, Garrigou rejects the ontological argument. Instead, the arguments for God's existence will be *a posteriori* and involve an inference from various, non-self-explanatory features of the world to a transcendent cause, the God of the philosophers. Each of these makes reference to the principle of causality, i.e. whatever is not cause of itself is caused by another, which in turn is a further specification of the Principle of Sufficient Reason, i.e. whatever actually exists has a sufficient reason/explanation for its existence. Since the PSR (as it is usually called) is a first principle, it cannot be proved; however, Garrigou argues that it can be proven indirectly by reduction to the Principle of Non-Contradiction, one of the traditional "three laws of thought" that one can deny only on pain of incoherence.

Garrigou then reconstructs the "five ways" (from motion, change, contingency, degrees of being and finality) in accordance with a common schema, generally called the Cosmological Argument: *The world necessarily demands a primary extrinsic cause; we call the primary extrinsic cause of the world God; therefore, God exists.*[2] Garrigou emphasizes that the notion of "cause" employed here is analogical rather than univocal. Since God is a transcendent being, no term used of creatures can literally apply to God except in a purely formal sense specifiable solely in relation to an effect as that which brings it about, makes it exist or occur, one broad enough to encompass modes of causality that share

---

[1] All references will be to the fifth edition, translated by Dom Bede Rose, St. Louis, Herder and Herder, 1934.

[2] Garrigou, 234. This version of the argument is not one of the five ways and is not further developed by Garrigou.

nothing in common with regard to their operation. Thus, the term 'cause' as it functions in the proof has merely extensional rather than a common intensional meaning; this, however, is sufficient to prevent the syllogistic argument for God's existence from containing four terms. Garrigou also insists that, although the descriptions under which each proof arrives at God (the prime mover, the uncaused cause, necessary being, perfect being and final cause of the universe) are all abstract and philosophical, they all converge on a single being, the God of the Philosophers, who is arguably also the God of living religion.

In obedience to Vatican I, mainstream neo-Thomism committed itself to the project of providing valid and sound proofs for God's existence that could be declined only on pain of self-contradiction, thus claiming to able to prove God's existence with certainty. It was this claim that attracted the brunt of criticism from the newly emerging movement known as analytic philosophy.

Analytic Philosophy

The philosophical movement known as Analytic Philosophy emerged out of British neo-Realism around the turn the twentieth century in the work of G. E. Moore (1873–1958) and Bertrand Russell (1872–1970); Moore's *Principia Ethica* (1903) is arguably the first classic work of the analytic tradition. Friends from their Cambridge days, where both would become teachers, Moore converted Russell from the fashionable Hegelianism of the day and recruited him for the neo-Realist camp. However, as time went on Moore and Russell diverged, establishing the two main traditions within analytic philosophy. The first of these traditions, associated with Russell, the young Wittgenstein and later, Logical Positivism, grounds philosophical analysis in modern mathematical or symbolic logic and applies that logic to the analysis of terms and propositions in ordinary language. The second, associated with Moore, the later Wittgenstein and what became known as Oxford Philosophy, emphasizes the informal logic or grammar of ordinary language as it functions in everyday contexts as a means of untying the conceptual knots that give rise to philosophical confusion. Both versions of analytic philosophy enjoyed success in the U.S., but the former tradition remained dominant.

Despite these divergent traditions, analytic philosophers shared certain themes in common. First, there was a commitment to the analysis of language as the primary task of the philosopher as opposed to the discussion and resolution of substantive philosophical questions. Indeed, analytic philosophy has often been associated (in the cases of Logical Positivism and Oxford Philosophy, for example) with deflationary programs intended to show how the traditional philosophical problems arise from linguistic confusion and can be dissolved or eliminated using the techniques of analytic philosophy. Secondly, analytic philosophers tended to see themselves as just one academic specialist among others, using a unique set of tools or skills to address largely formal problems and willingly abandoning all substantive questions to the special sciences. Thirdly, they tended to oscillate between seeing themselves either as "underlaborers" to the special sciences, using logical techniques to clear up methodological or conceptual problems associated with the natural and the social sciences or as engaged in "second-order" investigations of the questions that arise from reflection upon the discourse and practice of researches engaged in "first-order" empirical research. The main exception to this was the philosophy of language, which was regarded as the special province of philosophers and carried on without any special reference to linguistics or psychology until well into the late twentieth century. Fourthly, and most relevant here, analytic philosophers tended to have an adversarial relationship with traditional schools of philosophy, especially those, such as Idealism and neo-Thomism, that take the task of the philosopher to be the construction of a grand theory or world-view intended to integrate all of human knowledge and experience into a single totality. Analytic philosophers actively set about debunking such approaches as a way of demonstrating the superiority of their analytic techniques.

In general, the tenor of early analytic philosophy was hostile to religion in general and to theism in particular. Both Moore and Russell were irreligious and, though officially agnostic on the question of God's existence clearly regarded it as unlikely that there is a God. Most of the first generation of analytic atheists (such as A. J. Ayer, Antony Flew and Paul Edwards) came out of the logical positivist tradition and challenged the very intelligibility of the central claims of theism using the verifiability criterion of meaning. This appears to be largely an historical accident, however; there is nothing central to the analytic approach that requires irreligion or anti-supernaturalism. Near the end of the twentieth century, many theistic philosophers adopted the techniques and doctrines of analytic philosophy to mount new defence of the rationality of religious belief. We will see more of that below; for now, let us consider the shape of analytic atheism.

Analytic Atheism and the Meaningfulness of Religious Language

Early analytic atheist critiques of religion largely challenged the intelligibility or cognitive significance of God-talk on the ground that claims about God were neither capable of being verified nor falsified in sense-experience. Using various versions of the doctrines of verifiability and/or falsifiability, analytic philosophers urged that no literal sense or meaning could be attached to claims such as "There is a God" or "God loves us" and proposed analyses of religious language according to which the apparent substantive content of such claims could be explained as expressions of feeling or moral commitment. Let us briefly look at some of the developments in this area.

After the First World War, the movement known as Logical Positivism emerged in Germany and Austria. The Logical Positivists combined the new logic, pioneered by Frege and Russell, with the scientism of the older positivism: the result was a powerful critique of traditional philosophy, especially of the speculative metaphysics that had dominated European thought in the nineteenth century. This critique crystallized around what became known as the *verifiability criterion of meaningfulness* according to which a synthetic or factual proposition is meaningful only if is either verifiable or falsifiable in principle by reference to sense-experience. In the English-speaking world, the case for logical positivism was forcefully pressed by A. J. Ayer (1910–1989) in his book *Language, Truth and Logic*, published in 1936. Ayer did not hesitate to draw the obvious implications of verificationism for religious belief: since no sense-experience is relevant to the truth or the falsity of claims about God, such claims ultimately can have no literal meaning. As such, such claims are not genuine synthetic propositions after all and cannot be either true or false.

Although Logical Positivism had lost its cachet by the early 1950's, the sort of critique of religious language suggested by Positivism continued to be pressed. In attempting to explain the difference between the perspective of the believer and the non-believer with regard to God's existence, John Wisdom had suggested a parable about two persons who differ about whether or not a gardener tends a particular plot of uninhabited land.[1] On the one hand, there is apparent evidence of the plot's being tended, but not so much as to be overwhelming, leading one person to postulate a gardener while the other chalks it up to coincidence. As each attempt to confirm the existence of the gardener fails, the believer modifies his account until it ultimately amounts to the claim that an invisible, undetectable gardener tends the plot. At this point, says Wisdom, there is no longer a factual dispute between the two persons, although they may continue to try to convince each other of their respective positions.

While Wisdom was willing to leave the matter as it stands, Antony Flew (b. 1921) saw in Wisdom's parable a way to revive the Positivist critique of religious language. According to Flew, what the believer in Wisdom's parable does is progressively evacuate all meaning from his initial claims in order to avoid refutation. He starts with a fairly robust, ordinary conception of what the gardener is – an ordinary human being who tends the plot – but, as evidence fails to turn up to confirm the existence of that individual, he "explains" that failure by modifying his original claim about the nature and character of the gardener, ultimately casting it in such a way that no empirical evidence is any longer relevant to either the confirmation or falsification of that claim. In the same way, religious believers are ultimately forced by e.g., the evil we observe in the world to characterize God in such a way that nothing can count decisively either for or against the existence of that being. This may insulate belief in God from empirical refutation, but only at the cost evacuating religious claims of any factual content. If this is so, then either the claims of religion are meaningless or they are obviously false.

Flew's 900-word paper "Theology and Falsification", first published in *University* in 1950, is arguably the founding document of analytic philosophy of religion and evoked a great deal of discussion.[2] Indeed, the problem of the meaningfulness of religious language largely dominated philosophy of religion for the next two decades. Among philosophers persuaded by Flew's position, the project was to account for the use or function of religious language without

---
1   "Gods", *Proceedings of the Aristotelian Society*, 1944–5.
2   Reprinted in *New Essays in Philosophical Theology* (1955), 99–100.

granting it any cognitive content. Of the numerous non-cognitivist accounts of religious language, the prescriptivism of R. B. Braithwaite is typical.[1] Although religious claims have the grammatical form of factual statements, their lack of falsifiability rules out the possibility that they could be either true or false; nevertheless, religious language does not appear to be merely a string of vacuous sounds. Braithwaite's suggestion is that religious language is really a set of disguised prescriptions indicating a commitment to a particular way of life. Later exponents of this view, such as the Wittgensteinian D. Z. Phillips, treat religion itself as a "language game" constituting a "form of life" incommensurable to competing "forms of life", incapable of being either appreciated or critiqued from any neutral, external viewpoint and thus capable of being understood only from the point of view of the committed believer.[2]

Of course, the analytic philosophers were hardly the first to discuss the question of the meaningfulness of religious language. A long tradition of discussion of these matters going back at least to the time of the Pseudo-Dionysius (6th century CE) had struggled with the question of how human language can be used to describe the transcendent God.[3] One line of thought, popular in Eastern Orthodox, Jewish and Muslim theology, embraced the *via negativa*, according to which God is literally indescribable in human language such that we can only know what God is not rather than what God is and it is perhaps no surprise that in each of these traditions philosophy and theology were superseded by mysticism. In modern times, the symbolic interpretation of religious language developed by Paul Tillich echoes this tradition, but without its completion in the mystical apprehension of the ineffable God, who remains beyond any sort of human conception or encounter. Such views easily lend themselves to the sort of deflationary analysis of religious language proposed by Flew and Braithwaite.

Neo-Thomist thought, rooted in a tradition that goes back to the fifteenth century, interprets Thomas's position on this question as involving a distinction between three kinds of terms that can be applied to things: univocal, which are applied with exactly the same meaning, equivocal, which are applied with

---

[1] See "An Empiricist's view of the Nature of Religious Belief", *British Academy Lectures,* no. 9 (1955), 1–31.
[2] See, for example, Phillips (1966).
[3] See his *On the Divine Names* in Colm Luibheld, translator, *Pseudo-Dionysius: The Complete Works* (1987) 47–131.

completely diverse meanings, and *analogical*, applied with *different but related* meanings.[1] The term "extension", when applied to bodies, is used univocally. The term "bank", when used to apply both to the side of a riverbed and a financial institution, is used equivocally. The term "fast", when used to apply both to a friend and to a dye, is used equivocally, according to this tradition: clearly, there is an analogy between what it means to be a fast friend and a fast dye but this cannot be cashed out in any literal similarity of relation. The positive predicates used to describe God are to be understood of Him in just such a way: God is being, goodness, power and so on but His mode of possessing these characteristics shares nothing materially in common with those characteristics as possessed by creatures. In this manner we can make positive attributions to God without making religious language literally descriptive of God in such a way as to reduce God to something comparable to human beings.

The analytic atheists rejected this view, largely on the basis of descriptions of it given in Scholastic textbooks. Not surprisingly, they attacked the very idea of irreducibly analogical terms on grounds of vagueness; indeed, the analytic emphasis on clarity of meaning made the notion of such terms intolerable. Their standard criticism can be given in the form of a dilemma: either there is a common element in the meaning of these two terms, in which case they are at least partially univocal and thus not irreducibly analogical, or there is no specifiable element of common meaning, in which case the terms are equivocal after all and thus not irreducibly analogical. Although a number of philosophers have continued to defend the analogical theory, it has largely shared the fate of neo-Thomism generally.

This does not mean theistic philosophers have abandoned the field, however. At least two notable defences of the meaningfulness of religious language appeared in the 1960's and helped turn the tide against verificationism. The first of these, developed by John Hick, became known as eschatological verification: admitting that religious claims could not be falsified by sense-experience, Hick maintained that they were at least *in principle* verifiable by post-mortem experience. One can envisage the possibility that one experiences, after death, a new life in Heaven with God and His saints, thus confirming the beliefs of the

---

1   For a clear and perspicuous presentation of this doctrine, see Mascall (1949)

Christian religion.[1] Although rejected by some critics as inadequate because it makes essential reference to irreducibly religious ideas, most philosophers are nowadays willing to admit that religious claims are at least meaningful, even if entirely false.

A second, more recondite strategy was developed by a number of British theologians, the most prominent of whom was Ian Ramsey, later Bishop of Durham.[2] For Ramsey, the problem of using human language to describe God is essentially the problem of using a natural language derived from everyday, finite experience to describe a transcendent object and this problem is not unique to theology. For instance, in theoretical physics we have to use sense-experience as the basis for the theoretical understanding of the physical world which largely transcends that experience and which, modern science tells us, is radically different than the way it appears to us in sense-experience. Scientific theories, then, take the form of both mathematical and analogue models in which sets of equations and bodies of concepts are taken to be descriptive of transcendent realities to which they are structurally isomorphic. In a like manner, our vain attempts to make the self or ego an object lead us to recognize that the self is irreducibly subject, present in experience as that which experiences yet at the same time as transcendent to experience understood as objective mental content. By the same token, we spontaneously interpret the observable "behaviour" of other persons as the products of a conscious activity that transcends our experience *in principle* and thereby attribute to them an internal mental life qualitatively like our own. In all these cases, then, we use language to *disclose* or *direct attention to* realities that transcend sense-experience but which are nevertheless capable of being analogically modelled in thought.

Religious language functions in a similar way. There are various experiences that occur in the lives of ordinary human beings that function as "disclosure events" evoking the use of religious language to describe a dimly apprehended transcendent reality of central importance to human existence. There are many possible bases for such events; for example, even Hume thought that the order and apparent design of the universe ineluctably lead us to postulate the existence of a cosmic Designer. According to Ramsey, we go on to talk about the puta-

---

1   See Hick (1964).
2   See especially Ramsey (1967).

tive transcendent object disclosed in such experiences using *qualified models* in which a term normally and literally applicable to human beings or other observable entities is applied to God using an adjective that tips us off that the word is being used in an extended or non-standard sense, one required by the differences between that transcendent object and the standard case from which the term is derived. Thus, God is called "first cause", "supreme being", "absolute will" and so on; the qualifying adjectives are used to point to or indicate an aspect of disclosure experiences, i.e. that the object revealed by those experiences is different in kind from the other sorts of beings to which those terms can be applied.

For whatever reasons, as verificationism receded from prominence in the philosophy of language, so too did the Positivist and crypto-Positivist critiques of religious language. By the early 1970s, philosophers were once again eager to grapple with the substantive truth-claims of religion and, in particular, the question of God's existence and the problem of evil. Let us then return to the development of analytic atheism on this issue up to that time.

Atheistic Deductivism

In the mid-1960s, the atheistic critique of religious belief had developed a "two-pronged" approach consisting of two convergent strategies: *negative* and *positive* atheism.[1] Negative atheism is the philosophical critique of theism intended to show that there are no positive reasons or arguments sufficient to justify belief in God. Typically, this was done by showing that there are no valid and sound deductive proofs for God's existence. Negative atheism is, as the name implies, not committed to the defence of any positive thesis; however, this strategy generally takes atheism to be the default position in the debate over God's existence, such that the failure of theists to provide such proofs is enough to demonstrate the irrationality of religious belief. Positive atheism proposes to demonstrate the falsity of theism by means of positive arguments, ideally by means of deductive disproofs of God's existence showing that the concept of the theistic God is self-contradictory or incoherent. The negative atheist strategy was centrally focussed on the critique of the traditional arguments for God's existence, especially the "five ways", which (as we have seen) were routinely presented as deductively

---

1   See Martin (1991), 26 and 77–8 for a bare statement of this distinction.

valid and sound proofs for God's existence. The positive atheist strategy was centred on the deductive Argument from Evil. Let us briefly consider each of these critiques.

Atheistic Critique of the Five Ways

As we have seen, the mainstream manualist tradition in neo-Thomism asserted that the five ways were valid and sound deductive proofs for God's existence capable of yielding rational certainty of the existence of God apart from any specifically religious claims. This is a bold claim and one that the analytic atheists insisted that the neo-Thomists make good on pain of irrationality. However, the usual focus of the analytic atheist critique was a generalized version of the cosmological argument that infers from the existence of contingent beings to the existence of a First Cause which "everybody calls God." The criticisms of this sort of argument were generally just updated versions of the objections offered by Hume and Kant to traditional versions of this argument. To the supposition that individual contingent things (such as oneself) require a First Cause in order to exist, analytic atheists countered by supposing that this could be explained by a temporally-extended infinite regress of such beings, each of which is caused by a previous member of the series. To the claim that the whole series of such beings needs a cause, the response was made that if every member of the series can be accounted for in terms of another member of the series, this is sufficient to account for the series as well. The use of the PSR to motivate the postulation of a First Cause was also challenged on the ground that either the PSR applies to the First Cause – in which case *contra* hypothesis that First Cause will require a cause in its own case – or the existence of the First Cause is postulated as a surd fact requiring no explanation, in which case we may as well stop at the physical universe. Analytic atheists accused the neo-Thomists of various logical errors and fallacies as well; however, seemingly the final blow to the Thomistic version of the cosmological argument (coinciding with the aftermath of the Second Vatican Council) was Anthony Kenny's book *The Five Ways*, in which Kenny (b. 1926; now Sir Anthony) argues that Aquinas' arguments for God's existence presuppose the Aristotelian physical picture in such a manner that his arguments cannot be usefully reconstructed apart from it, and thus must be seen as superseded by the scientific account of the world.[1] Of course, the analytic atheists also used the traditional Humean/Kantian criticisms to reject the teleological and ontological arguments as well; however, given that neo-Thomism was, at the time, the only organized school of theistic philosophers it is not surprising that the Cosmological argument was the primary focus of atheistic critique. Nor does this mean that interest in (or the defence of) traditional arguments for God's existence altogether disappeared after the onslaught of the analytic atheists. We will pick this thread up in the last chapter of this essay; for now let us turn to the positive atheist critique of theism represented by the deductive argument from evil.

The Argument from Evil

In 1955, J. L. Mackie published his classic paper "Evil and Omnipotence," initiating the contemporary debate about the problem of evil.[2] Mackie takes it for granted that the classical arguments for God's existence have all been refuted; he worries, however, that theists may attempt to evade the necessity of atheism by appealing to faith as the foundation for religious belief. In order to cut off this last resort, Mackie proposes to show that the concept of the theistic God is incoherent. According to Mackie, traditional theism has three non-negotiable commitments:

1. God is omnipotent.
2. God is omniscient.
3. God is morally perfect.

However, according to Mackie, these three propositions become part of an inconsistent set of propositions when conjoined to

4. Evil exists.

If God is omnipotent, then He has the power to prevent all evil. If He is omniscient, then He cannot plead ignorance. It remains that either God lacks these two qualities or else is deficient in benevolence. On any of these options, the theistic God is non-existent.

---

[1] New York, Shocken Books, 1970.
[2] Originally published in the *Australasian Journal of Philosophy* (1955); reprinted in Pike, *God and Evil*, 1965, 46–60.

Mackie spends the bulk of his article examining and rejecting various defences that theists might propose to blunt the force of the argument. It is not plausible to either suppose that evil is non-existent or to weaken the idea of God to suggest that God is finite. Neither is there any good for which the possibility of evil is a necessary condition (such as free will or the exemplification of virtue) that outweighs the evil that we observe in the world. Mackie concludes that theism is intellectually bankrupt and that belief in God is an exercise in wilful irrationality, at least among the educated.

Many other analytic atheist philosophers endorsed Mackie's argument and attempted to provide additional support for it.[1] Although there were responses on behalf of the theist, the argument seemed to carry everything before it when it first appeared. With the apparent success of the argument from evil, the circle seemed to be closed and the final nail driven into the coffin of religious belief; from within the ambit of the deductivist approach to the philosophy of religion, it appeared that there were no further defences of theism available and no prospect of showing that religious belief could be intellectually respectable. Of course, it would be incorrect to suggest that discussion of the proofs for God's existence or the construction of theodicies was wholly abandoned. Nevertheless, the general consensus among philosophers during the 1960's was decidedly atheistic. Here our story might have ended, and undoubtedly would have ended if the first generation of analytic atheists had had their way. Surprisingly, however, it turns out that it was only the beginning of a story that it will take the rest of this essay to tell.

---

1   See H. J. McCloskey's essay, reprinted in Pike (1965) 51–84 and Scriven (1966) Chapter 4, 87–167.

Chapter Three

Inductivism

In 1960, Nelson Pike published his paper "Hume on Evil" which ultimately proved to be as influential as Mackie's "Omnipotence and Evil."[1] Taking his cue from the deductivist interpretation of Mackie's argument, Pike argued that theism would be vindicated if one were able to remove the apparent contradiction between the traditional conception of God and the fact of evil. Pike proposes that the following will be sufficient to do the trick:

> 5. God has a good reason for permitting evil.

It is certainly *possible* that proposition 5 is true; if that is so, there is no formal contradiction in propositions 1–4 above. As such, the threat of the deductive argument from evil is removed. Pike emphasizes that his point is purely formal; it stands whether or not the theist can claim, even in principle, to know what the reason might be that would justify an omnipotent, omniscient and morally perfect being in permitting evil. Pike predicted that the problem of evil, construed as Mackie's argument typically was, would soon be seen to be a relatively minor challenge to theism. He was wrong, of course; the problem of evil remains a major topic of discussion even today. Nevertheless, Pike's refutation of the deductive argument from evil (repeated since by many other philosophers) had its effect; the claim to be able to deductively disprove God's existence from the fact of evil was quietly dropped by the 1970's. Further, no fewer than two paradigms in the

---

[1] Originally published in the *Philosophical Review*, 1960; reprinted in *God and Evil*, 1965, 85–102.

philosophy of religion take their fountainhead from Pike's seminal article. The first, Inductivism, was initiated by atheistic philosophers of religion in response to Pike's critique of Mackie and will be the subject of this chapter. The second, post-Deductivism, will be the subject of the next chapter.

One natural response to Pike's argument is to suggest that, while the existence of God might be barely logically possible, it is not plausible to suppose that there might exist any reason that would justify an omnipotent, omniscient and omnibenevolent being in permitting evil, and admittedly it is difficult to imagine what such a reason might be off the top of one's head. This naturally led to a new version of the argument from evil, according to which the fact of evil makes God's existence *improbable*, indeed so improbable as to make it beneath rational credence. As Hume puts it, a wise man apportions belief to evidence. Even if one cannot deductively disprove God's existence by reference to the fact of evil, one can still argue that the fact of evil, or perhaps its amount or its manner of distribution, provides overwhelming inductive evidence against God's existence. Thus, while one cannot be convicted of the sort of positive irrationality that involves believing a contradiction, one can at least be accused of irrationality in some further sense that involves the violation of some generally recognized and applicable principle of doxastic responsibility we use in forming and maintaining beliefs, such as the Humean principle just articulated. The theist, then, is hardly out of the woods and evil still remains a formidable challenge to the propriety of theistic belief.

One obvious response to this challenge would be to engage in classical theodicy, i.e. the enterprise of attempting to provide a reason or set of reasons that plausibly explain, at least in general, why a being like the theistic God would allow evils of the sort and amount that we observe in the world. Generalizing this response, one could argue, given the total evidence relevant to the question of God's existence, that even if theism does look improbable given the facts about evil in the world, this evidence is counterbalanced and outweighed by the positive evidence for God's existence derived from other considerations. The question, then, concerns the *reasonableness* of theistic belief on the total body of empirical evidence relevant to the judgment concerning God's existence and one can claim that God's existence is reasonable, according to relevant standards for reasonable belief applicable to the situation, without being able to claim to categorically *prove* that God exists or demonstrate the positive irrationality of disbelief. Once we have reached this perspective, we have arrived at the Inductivist paradigm in the philosophy of religion.

Mitchell's Inductivist Proposal

In 1973, Basil Mitchell published *The Justification of Religious Belief*,[1] in which he outlined the Inductivist approach to the evaluation and defence of religious belief, of which belief in God will, of course, be one significant component. According to Mitchell, there are many contexts in which it is not possible to adjudicate substantive claims on the basis of apodictic proof; indeed, outside of logic and mathematics, it is the rule rather than the exception for any significant question to be settled by deductive proofs. In the natural and social sciences, in history and literary criticism we are largely stuck with hypotheses that are incapable of any sort of conclusive proof. Further, given what contemporary philosophers and historians of science have taught us about the process of "paradigm change" in the natural sciences and the inconclusive nature of traditional ideas of confirmation and falsification, we have come to appreciate the role of other, non-traditional measures of credibility and the existence of a number of dimensions in the evaluation of hypotheses. The central role played by epistemic conservativism, considerations of simplicity, comprehensiveness, fecundity and coherence in the evaluation of potential theories is now widely recognized, as well as the legitimacy of appeals to such considerations in deciding between hypotheses. According to Mitchell, this changed appreciation of the nature of theory-acceptance in science (and in other disciplines) has equal significance for metaphysics and apologetics as well. Negatively, the demand that theologians prove God's existence by some sort of apodictic rational proof can be seen as unreasonable when we routinely reject such a standard in every other discipline that deals with substantive questions about the nature of reality. Positively, we can reconceive the apologetic task as more like the interpretation of a cultural practice, an historical event or the meaning of a poem, enterprises with a substantive upshot capable of being rationally evaluated though not, perhaps, in the way we standardly do in the "hard" sciences. Mitchell then goes on to sketch, in

---

1 See Mitchell (1973) *passim*.

outline, how this might be done.

For Mitchell, Christian theism ought to be viewed as a *world-hypothesis*, an overarching, comprehensive "theory of everything" intended to account for the most general and pervasive features of reality as we experience it in everyday life and understand it through natural science. As such, theism competes with other, contrary world-hypotheses, such as metaphysical naturalism, idealism, Buddhist nihilism, etc. Since all of these world-hypotheses are general and comprehensive, they cannot be tested empirically by observation or experiment, nor is there any reason to suppose that novelty evidence will emerge that will tip the scales in favour of one world-hypothesis as opposed to another. However, according to Mitchell, this no more rules out rational judgments of relative plausibility in the case of world-hypotheses than it does in the case of historical or literary interpretation. Instead, one must proceed by constructing a *cumulative case* that draws from a broad range of phenomena functioning as data that together provide support for the Christian theist worldview and then arguing that Christian theism gives the overall best account of the data relative to competitors. In evaluating this claim, the same sorts of criteria for judgement apply as apply in the disciplines mentioned above: simplicity, coherence, empirical fit, comprehensiveness, fecundity, illumination and so on. Of course, the construction of such a case and its evaluation will not be easy or probably as clear-cut as we would like. Nevertheless, we can at least hope that Christian theism will emerge as a plausible view well above the threshold of rational credence.

In Mitchell's case, this remains only a hope; he does not go on, in *The Justification of Religious Belief*, to actually undertake the arduous task of attempting to construct such a cumulative case. Mitchell leaves that project to others; nevertheless, his book represents a major strategic shift in theistic apologetics, one that others were soon to take up, in particular Richard Swinburne.

Swinburne's Bayesian Theism

The most important exponent of the inductivist approach from within theism is Richard Swinburne (b. 1931) who in a series of books beginning in 1979 articulates a complete theistic philosophy of religion that itself amounts in effect to a complete philosophical system.¹ It is Swinburne who, more than anyone else, has realized the promise of the inductivist paradigm in the philosophy of religion. If Swinburne has not had more followers it is only perhaps because (as a church chorister once said of a particularly loud tenor) "he leaves nothing for the rest of us to do." Swinburne's impressive *oeuvre*, which includes over a dozen books in the philosophy of religion alone, cannot receive but the sketchiest summary here; the reader is encouraged to investigate his works for him- or herself. Nevertheless, I hope to present enough of an outline to at least provide a general idea of his approach.

Within the Inductivist paradigm, the question of whether or not God's existence can be proved is replaced with that of whether or not belief in God is *reasonable*. The natural suggestion is that it is possible for a belief to be reasonable, at least for some persons under some circumstances, without those persons possessing apodictic proof of the truth of that belief. This conforms to what happens to be the case about most of our common-sense beliefs, for example. Still, one would like to have some account of what makes a belief reasonable for someone in those circumstances in which conclusive proof for that belief is unavailable.

One way of articulating the notion of reasonableness is in terms of *probability*. A belief may be probable relative to the evidence for that belief, hence reasonable to believe, even if the evidence falls short of conclusive proof, just so long as the evidence confers a probability sufficient to make that belief credible according to the standards applicable in the circumstances in which the belief is up for consideration. One intuitive way to measure sufficiency in this context would be by reference to the mathematical calculus of probability, according to which any belief that has a probability greater than .5 relative to the evidence, being more likely to be true than not, is reasonable to believe, and the higher the probability above that, the more reasonable it will be to believe. By contrast, beliefs with probability less than .5 relative to the evidence, being less likely to be true than their denials, will not be reasonable to believe and those with probability equal to .5, being neither less nor more likely to be true than their denials, will be those about which it is best to suspend judgment. Something like this

---

1   Here my presentation will follow Swinburne's *The Existence of God*, 2ⁿᵈ Edition (2004); See my *Analytic Philosophy of Religion* for a more comprehensive account of Swinburne's views based on the whole corpus of his writings.

idea lies behind Swinburne's Inductivist defence of theism.

However, there are a number of different theories of probability and these theories differ about what kinds of considerations are relevant to judgements of probability and how these are to be measured. From early on, Swinburne embraced the Bayesian account of probability, according to which potential beliefs are treated as hypotheses and the probabilities of such beliefs are taken to be the function of their intrinsic (or *prior*) probability combined with their probability given the available evidence, taking into account the probability that the evidence might have obtained regardless of the truth of that hypothesis and the probability that the denial of that belief might be true on the same evidence. The prior probability of a belief is its probability on no evidence whatever and it is a characteristic feature of Bayesian probability theory that hypotheses have prior probabilities, such that it is possible for two hypotheses to have different probabilities prior to the examination of evidence. For Swinburne, the prior probability of any hypothesis is determined by its simplicity. Once the prior probability of a hypothesis has been determined, we then look at the available evidence in order to determine the probability of that hypothesis relative to the data; that, multiplied by the prior probability, gives us the posterior probability of that hypothesis considered in itself. We discover the objective probability of the hypothesis by dividing the amount of the first calculation with the combined probabilities of that evidence obtaining even if the hypothesis is false and the probability that the hypothesis might be false on that evidence. If the final result gives us a probability greater than .5, then the hypothesis in question is more likely than not to be true, hence reasonable to believe; if the final result gives us a probability less than .5, it is less likely than not to be true, hence not reasonable to believe.

While the Bayesian account of probability gives us a framework for making rational judgements about what to believe, it works best in those cases in which it is possible for us to assign actual numerical values to the components of the calculation. As Swinburne himself ultimately came to admit, there is no prospect of making any such (non-arbitrary) assignments in the case of God's existence. Nevertheless, Swinburne maintains that the Bayesian approach can support the intuitive judgement that, given the prior probability of theism and its probability relative the to available evidence, it is more likely than not that theism is true, despite the facts that a world such as ours could have been produced by chance and that the existence of evil in the world has to be reckoned evidence against the hypothesis that God exists. On the basis of this intuitive judgement that it is reasonable to believe that God exists, we therefore infer that God's existence is more likely than not, hence that the probability that God exists is greater than .5, on the grounds that to believe a proposition is to believe that it is true, hence that it is more likely to be true than not, which entails believing that its probability is greater than .5.

Swinburne maintains that where the evaluation of hypotheses is concerned, novelty evidence plays no essential role in determining whether or not a hypothesis is likely to be true or false. As such, it is not essential for any hypothesis to be the object of serious consideration that it is either confirmable or falsifiable by reference to either predictions about future experience or postdictions concerning what we might discover about past events. He labels as *predictivism* the prejudice in favour of "testable" as opposed to "non-testable" hypotheses, urging that it is the performance of the hypotheses relative to the whole body of available evidence, rather than simply with regard to novelty evidence, that determines the likelihood that the hypothesis is true. This has obvious application in the case of theism, since it is unlikely that there will be any novelty evidence that will turn up to resolve the question of whether or not God exists.

Having sketched Swinburne's methodology, we will now consider his case for theism, in three stages. First, we will consider Swinburne's account of the prior probability of theism. Second, we will outline Swinburne's positive case for theism by reference to the evidence that favours a theistic interpretation of reality. Thirdly and finally, we will consider his theodicy, given in aid of reducing the degree to which the fact of evil provides evidence against the claim that God exists.

Swinburne on the Prior Probability of Theism

According to Swinburne, simplicity is the proper measure of the prior probability of a worldview. In fact, according to Swinburne, all of the criteria we use to evaluate the likely truth of hypotheses ultimate reduce to or are aspects of simplicity. Taking this as his starting point, Swinburne compares theism to two rival conceptions of the universe and argues that theism is preferable to both on grounds of simplicity, hence has a higher intrinsic probability than those rivals. According to theism, the ultimate explanation of everything is to be found in the intellect and will of God, the Supreme Being; thus, the categories of personal explanation serve as the ground of inanimate explanation. According to materialism, the ultimate explanation of everything is to be found in the operation of inanimate matter, to which thought and intentional behaviour must somehow be reduced or else explained away. According to what Swinburne calls humanism both personalistic and inanimate explanation are equally fundamental and neither is reducible to the other or explicable in terms of the other.

Swinburne argues that theism and materialism are superior to humanism on grounds of simplicity, since each of these theories postulates a single ultimate principle of explanation, whereas humanism postulates two such principles both of which are equally independent yet fortuitously present in the world and complementary to each other. Swinburne then argues that theism is superior to materialism insofar as it postulates a single, simple entity, God, as its ultimate explanatory principle whereas the materialist is forced to postulate the entire physical universe, i.e. matter, the laws governing matter, and the results of the operation of those laws, as a surd fact about reality. Interestingly enough, Swinburne does not try to argue that God's existence is self-explanatory or take refuge in the notion that God is a necessary being in the sense of a being whose non-existence is impossible. All ultimate explanation involves the postulation of a surd fact or facts, so that if it is the ultimate fact about the universe, then the fact that God exists is a surd fact. The reason for postulating God rather than the material universe as the ultimate surd fact is simply that it is ontologically simpler. To the objection that we observe the physical universe but not God, Swinburne would no doubt respond that at this point we are simply considering a choice between world-hypotheses as such without reference to the actual state of our knowledge. Given this context, we are thereby able to fix the intrinsic probability of each of these hypotheses. That theism outperforms its rivals in this context is certainly encouraging, but it is hardly the last word on the subject. This sets up the next stage of the inquiry.

Swinburne's Positive Case for Theism

In his book *The Existence of God*, Swinburne outlines the positive case for theistic belief, arguing that the theistic hypothesis explains certain broad and pervasive facts about and features of the universe better than its materialist rival by supposing that they are the expression of the decisions of an intentional agent who formed the universe in accordance with an overall plan. While each of the lines of evidence are independent of one another, each is also complementary to the others and while none of these features of the universe is enough, by itself, to make it more likely than not that God exists, taken together they constitute a good inductive argument for God's existence which does raise the probability of God's existence to significantly higher than .5. By contrast, the failure of materialism to account for these facts requires it to multiply the number of surd facts that it must countenance and the number of auxiliary hypotheses it must embrace in order to avoid theism, thus reducing both its explanatory power and its simplicity which in turn lowers its overall probability.

Swinburne goes on to note that, while just about any universe is compatible with the truth of materialism, theism makes fairly specific claims about the sort of universe that God would create. In particular, says Swinburne, a universe created by a theistic God would be one in which self-conscious, rational moral agents capable of knowing and loving God would exist, and universes of this sort represent only a small fraction of the possible universes that might exist. Given pure chance, that the universe should be one of the sort created we can anticipate the theistic God to create would be very low; if placed behind a Rawlsian "veil of ignorance" with regard to the nature of the actual world, we would be well-advised to bet against, rather than for, the idea that such a universe exists. Therefore, the very fact that the actual world is as we would expect it to be if God existed rather than if it were the product of blind chance is surprising and must be accounted as good inductive evidence for God's existence, i.e. evidence that raises the probability that theism is true higher than it was previously, i.e. higher than its intrinsic probability alone.

Swinburne then goes on to consider the traditional arguments for God's existence, considered now not as deductive proofs for God's existence, but instead as further lines of evidence, drawn from our general knowledge of the world, for the theistic hypothesis. For example, Swinburne finds a use for the traditional cosmological argument. We have, he says, no scientifically credible explanation for the existence of the universe and the physical laws governing that universe. The universe gives every appearance of being a collection of contingent beings, hence bids fair to be a contingent being itself, one that need never have existed, even if in fact it has existed for all eternity. There is no genuine sense to be attached to the notion that the universe might have simply "popped" into existence out of nothing and physical models intended to show how this is possible always end up postulating some complex pre-existent mechanism whose own existence is both inexplicable and unverifiable. Furthermore, the universe is too massive and its law-governed character to pronounced to make us comfortable in taking its existence as a surd fact in need of no further explanation. By contrast, however, an omnipotent, omniscient and benevolent deity is precisely the kind of being whose existence may plausibly be taken as a surd fact not requiring any further explanation. It is therefore quite reasonable for us to postulate God rather than the physical universe as we observe it to be ultimate reality. Thus, in the very existence of the universe we find a good inductive argument for God's existence.

The sorts of considerations that give rise to the teleological argument provide more arrows for Swinburne's quiver. On materialism, for example, we have very little reason to suppose that the universe would be highly ordered given that it is produced by merely random processes, since on that supposition only a small fraction of the possible universes could be expected to have this feature. The existence of a highly ordered universe is therefore highly unlikely on materialism; however, such a universe is precisely what we observe. One could say, of course, that highly unlikely events sometimes happen, but it hardly seems reasonable to accept this claim when an obvious candidate-explanation like theism is available: even if we reject the Principle of Sufficient Reason, we ought not to multiply surd facts and improbabilities in the face of long odds beyond necessity. Further, attempts to provide speculative physical or quasi-physical explanations that postulate an infinite number of universes or universe-generating mechanisms (such as "cosmic evolution" or "inflationary cosmology") to account for the appearance of having beaten the long odds through some combination of chance and necessity are inevitably more complex than the theistic hypothesis and have a decidedly *ad hoc* quality about them. Finally, appeal to the "anthropic principle", according to which it is not surprising that the universe is as we find it, since if it were not, we would not be here to wonder about it, falls flat; if my existence is due to a highly improbable set of occurrences, my surprise and wonder at that fact are hardly out of place.

Swinburne also notes that the sort or order and regularity that we observe in the universe, as well as its aesthetic properties, are what theism would "predict" about the universe. The universe displays both diachronic (temporal) and synchronic (spatial) order. Due to the former, both the behaviour of non-rational beings and the likely consequences of the actions of rational beings are knowable and predictable in advance, thus making it possible for rational beings to both understand and predict the course of the world, an ability that is perfected as time goes on. Due to the latter, a stable world-order underwriting the evolution and continued existence of embodied rational beings is both made possible and then subsequently realized, once again in the face of long odds when such a scenario is considered solely with regard to its intrinsic probability. In a like manner, the amazement and delectation we derive from the observation and study of nature are hardly to be expected on a materialist picture of things, but will be rather more likely to be present if the universe were the product of an intelligent creator. Given that God has as His end the creation of a universe in which self-conscious, rational moral agents capable of knowing and loving Him would exist, He would have good reason to include all of these features or order into His creation. So, once again, things are as we would expect them to be if theism were true; each of these considerations, then, constitutes a successful inductive argument for God's existence.

Again, neither consciousness nor conscious recognition of the moral law and moral obligation are to be expected in a materialist universe. Yet, despite this, one of the most evident facts available to each one of us is our status as self-conscious, rational moral agents. Not only is there no expectation that beings such as ourselves would ever exist if materialism is true, it is very difficult to see how beings such as ourselves would even be possible on the materialist picture of things. Consciousness, as experienced from the first-person perspective, consists of mental states to which we have privileged access and which are not physically observable; my self as embodied possesses physical properties which are publicly observable but not introspectible. While it is clear that there are causal connections running both ways from physical states of my brain to mental events in sense-perception and from mental states to states of my brain in the causation of intentional actions, the two kinds of states and my relations to them make very plausible the idea that what I am is a mental substance or soul that has a body rather than merely a material body as such. Swinburne enforces this idea by considering some thought experiments involving brain transplants. Suppose that a mad scientist divides my brain in half and transplants one half of it into one body and the other half into another. Which, if either of these, is me? If my mind/self were nothing but my brain, there ought to be an answer to this question, but in fact no matter how much we knew about my brain and no matter what subsequently happened, no one would ever be able to re-identify me on physical grounds alone. Therefore, concludes Swinburne, my self and my brain are not identical. Given this result, we ought to conclude that the self is not anything physical at all, but instead an immaterial substance or soul.

If the soul and the body are separate substances, the question remains how to explain the causal laws that govern the interaction of these two substances. Neither the body nor the soul can be the source or explanation of these laws and while evolution can explain why, once these mechanisms are in place, they should work the way they do to produce largely true beliefs, it is powerless to explain why such mechanisms should exist in the first place. It remains, then, that God must be their source, and to have dictated a set of laws that conduce to the overall success of his plan for the world which includes the existence of self-conscious rational moral agents as we know ourselves to be. Thus, the senses will have to serve both as a means to inform us of what is beneficial and harmful in our environment and to give us the data we need to understand the basic laws of nature and the processes they underwrite from a theoretical point of view, which in turn will indirectly subserve the goal of survival. God would thus have good reason for supplying us with these cognitive powers and this provides a good personalistic explanation for that fact; in turn, it supplies a further inductive argument for God's existence.

Swinburne, unlike many theistic philosophers, does not appeal to God as the source of the moral law; according to Swinburne, the basic laws of morality are necessary truths knowable *a priori*. At the same time, however, we have no reason to suppose that any natural process, including evolution, would endow us with a capacity for *a priori* knowledge or the faculty of conscience that allows us to feel the necessity of moral obligation in a manner that makes that knowledge action-guiding. The theistic God, however, would have good reason to see that this comes about, since these would be necessary conditions for the possibility of moral agency. So far forth, then, the world is as we would expect it to be if theism were true and not as we would expect it to be if materialism were true. So once again we have a good inductive argument for God's existence.

If God has endowed us with cognitive faculties for knowledge and moral agency, we can expect that God will put us in an environment in which the exercise of these faculties will be both possible and of significant import. It is appropriate that finite persons, both individually and collectively, should have scope for significant action, both in the pursuit of theoretical knowledge and in relation to their treatment of one another and that these activities should have a certain urgency about them. This will be best accomplished in an environment in which theoretical knowledge is possible for us but not necessarily easy to acquire and in which finite persons are vulnerable both to nature and to one another, thus giving us significant choices about how to treat those others and ourselves. Of course, Swinburne notes, this is the sort of environment in which we find ourselves, so once again the universe is as we would expect it to be if God existed; this gives us a further inductive argument for God's existence, one which Swinburne calls the Argument from Providence.

Swinburne rounds out his positive case for theism by appealing to religious experience and miracles. If the theistic God existed, He would have reason to reveal Himself to his rational creatures in a manner that respects their free will, for only in such case would a free, loving response to God be possible. Therefore, there is a high prior probability that people would report the occurrence of religious experience, acts of divine revelation and divine interventions in natural processes in response to human free choices at least in some circumstances. Of course, if atheists could prove that there is no God or that the prior probability of God was too low to take seriously, claims to this effect would not be worth taking seriously; however, to simply assume that this is the case would simply beg the question against theism. As such, the atheist cannot simply dismiss all claims to this effect out of hand.

With regard to such reports, Swinburne proposes that we should use the same principle to govern which claims to religious experience, revelation and miracles we take seriously as we use to evaluate questions of testimony in everyday life. Swinburne calls this the principle of credulity, which we may summarize as the claim that the *prima facie* best explanation for someone's claiming to have experienced X is that the person in question did in fact experience X. In accordance with this principle, we ought to regard such claims as likely to be true unless there are good reasons to suppose otherwise, such as that the witness was unreliable, the events reported were intrinsically improbable or that we subsequently discover that the putative occurrence was a purely natural event. Some claims regarding miracles and religious experience can be discounted in these ways; however, Swinburne is convinced that there are a great many such claims that cannot be. In the case of the Resurrection, for example, Swinburne has defended both the high intrinsic probability of God's witnessing to Christ's messianic status and the historicity of the Gospel accounts. Such claims cannot be simply dismissed on question-begging *a priori* grounds, as atheists are wont to do. Of course, if any such claims to stand up to scrutiny, they ought to be accepted as likely to be true just like any other claim based on testimony; these will constitute an additional inductive argument for God's existence.

Does Swinburne's review of the evidence tip the scales in favour of theism? Having presented ten or so independent inductive arguments for God's existence, he then goes on to argue that these, taken in conjunction with the fact that the intrinsic probability of theism is higher than its rivals and outperforms them in explaining the traditional evidences for God's existence, that it is reasonable to suppose that the cumulative force of the evidence raises the probability that God exists higher than .5, thus making theism reasonable to believe. However, before we can rest confidently in this result, we need to take into account the evidence against the existence of God represented by the fact of evil. Swinburne does so by providing a theodicy, an account of the likely reasons that God might have for permitting the evils we see around us in the world.

Swinburne's Theodicy

Swinburne agrees with Mackie and other atheists that the existence of evil in the world is *prima facie* evidence against theism and thus makes theism improbable so far forth. However, the question is whether or not the evidence against God's existence represented by evil counts decisively against theism, i.e. reduces its probability below .5. As we have seen, there is according to Swinburne a significant amount of positive evidence for theism and this must be taken into account in any fair assessment of the overall probability of theism. Furthermore, given the nature of that evidence, it is possible for us, says Swinburne, to construct a general account of some of the reasons that would justify God in permitting evil in the world, i.e. a partial theodicy capable of mitigating the evidential value of evil as evidence against God's existence by showing it to be less weighty than it first appears when looked at from a limited perspective that focuses solely on observed evils.

Swinburne first considers under what conditions a perfectly good and omnipotent God would be justified in permitting evils. Here Swinburne presents an analysis that is reminiscent of the Principle of Licit Double Effect. First of all, says Swinburne, God would be justified in permitting evil if it were either logically or morally impossible to bring about some great good without permitting such evils to occur. Secondly, God must ensure that the good for which the evil is a necessary condition actually obtains. Thirdly, the evils that God permits his creatures to suffer must be such that God has the right to impose them on creatures. Finally, says Swinburne, the evil permitted must not so outweigh the good for which that evil is a necessary condition that due proportionality fails to obtain.

If God has, as one of His legitimate ends in creating the world, the existence of self-conscious rational moral agents such as we take ourselves to be, we ought to expect that a significant variety and amount of both moral and natural evil should be observed in the world. If such agents are to have significant moral choices, then they need to possess free will and thus the power to misuse their free will to choose moral evil as well as moral good; thus, the possibility of moral evil is logically implicated in the very creation of such beings. Further, human beings will only have significant moral choices if the choices they make, whether for well or ill, are generally effective. A God who intervened to prevent every freely chosen evil from having its desired effect, or who even guaranteed that evil would be permitted only a certain point, would greatly diminish not only the scope but the seriousness of our moral choices, thus undermining the purpose for which He would have originally endowed us with free will.

By the same token, we will have significant responsibility for ourselves and others only if we, as embodied beings, are vulnerable and capable of affecting each other for well or ill in serious ways. For this it is required that there be natural evils capable of afflicting us against which we need to guard ourselves and others and which provide opportunities for us to tend the afflicted. Likewise, given our knowledge of our natural vulnerabilities, we are thereby made capable of helping, nurturing and protecting each other and given the opportunity to both develop and express such virtues as compassion, courage and so on. Of course, we can also act irresponsibly, run unreasonable risks or allow others to do so, fail to help, nurture and protect each other. Indeed, we can even use such knowledge to inflict positive harm on others for a variety of reasons. Once again, however, it is difficult to see how these possibilities can be eliminated without greatly diminishing the scope of our moral choices and, if their possibility is a necessary condition for this to be the case not even God can so act as to prevent them from being actualized through our free choices.

In order for us to acquire the knowledge relevant to making significant moral choices with regard to ourselves and others, the universe needs to be structured so that natural processes are largely predictable and morally neutral. Unless this was so, we would never be able to predict the outcomes of our actions with sufficient confidence to make rational decisions about what to do. Such knowledge, however, must be acquired inductively, through observation and experiment, so that the basic laws governing natural processes can be discovered and the likely consequences of our actions discerned. But not only does this knowledge make rational action possible, it also gives us the basic information by means of which we can anticipate and take steps to guard ourselves against natural evils. Suppose, for example, that a world suitable for rational beings such as ourselves requires that the surface of the Earth be formed by plate tectonics, one consequence of which is occasional but sometimes catastrophic volcanic eruptions, earthquakes and tsunamis. By studying these phenomena, we can learn how to predict these events with some accuracy, to make contingency plans prior to their occurrence, to retrofit our buildings and freeways and thus diminish the impact of such events when they occur. This knowledge, of course, comes at a price: earthquakes (etc.) must occur and people must die as a consequence, both in order to provide data for the scientific inquiry into the phenomena and the growth of technology and to motivate us to inquire in the first place.

None of the foregoing matters much unless God has the right to permit some persons to suffer in the first place. Certainly, it would not be right for one human being to make another suffer (without his or her consent, anyway) in order to benefit others or even the human race as a whole. At the same time, says Swinburne, parents have some limited right to impose (at least minor) deprivations and sufferings on their children for the sake of other family members or the family as a whole, because parents have a peculiar authority over their children due to the fact that they have brought them into existence and thereby acquired special responsibility for them. Since God is the creator of all things and there is nothing we possess that we have not received as a gift from Him, God has a corresponding parental authority over us which permits Him to permit us to suffer for the good of creation as a whole. Further, the sufferings we undergo are often redeemed by the good they make possible; in this way, God brings good out of evil. On either supposition, our sufferings, however apparently severe, are never pointless or in vain; to the contrary, they give us the opportunity to cooperate with God in accomplishing His ends in the world. God cannot ask us prior to making us whether or not we are willing to suffer to attain his ends; nor, prior to our actual existence, could we make any sort of sensible choice in the matter. Nevertheless, what God has freely given God can freely take away; gratitude for what we have been given ought to motivate us to freely return to God whatever He requires of us. Finally, God is unique in that He can compensate us, in the next life, for our sufferings in this to a degree far outweighing whatever loss they may represent to us. Thus, even a life of apparently unrelieved suffering is not a total loss if theism is true as it would be if our lives merely end with the grave.

Swinburne concludes his theodicy by considering three final issues. First, what about the pain suffered by animals? Swinburne suggests that this is a tricky matter inasmuch as we have very little evidence to go on as to either the nature or the amount of animal pain. Pain is obviously of great use to non-rational creatures as a means of governing their behaviour for their own benefit and it is at least possible that, while animals feel pain (experience painful sensations) they do not suffer as rational beings who feel pain often do. Further, Swinburne suggests, animals have limited capacities for knowledge and virtue in caring for each other and their progeny; so perhaps a limited version of the "greater goods" defence might also apply in their case as well. In a like manner, most of us believe that it is permissible for us to impose pain on animals (in e.g. medical experiments) in order to provide significant benefits for human beings (such as the discovery of insulin). Once again, God as the creator would have even greater right to do this for the greater good of the universe as a whole, even if animals do not have immortal souls.

Secondly, is there too much evil in the world? Swinburne feels the weight of this challenge most keenly; there does seem to be an awful lot of evil in the world, much more than what (from our limited point of view, at any rate) is necessary in order for the greater goods that evil makes possible to exist. At the same time, it is difficult to articulate this intuition as anything more than a complaint, since there is no objective standard or measure that we can employ in order to determine how much evil is enough and how much is too much. Swinburne reminds us that every evil that is eliminated is also an opportunity for good that is eliminated as well; if there were but few evils in the world that could be easily mastered, there would be correspondingly fewer opportunities to exercise agency, acquire virtue or benefit the human race through research and invention. It seems right, then, that there should be significant, persistent and challenging evils for us to combat; without them, life would lose much of its poignancy, seriousness and point. But this does not give us a ready answer as to why God would permit specific heinous evils, such as the Holocaust or the Black Death, so Swinburne admits that he has not entirely met the challenge of this objection: evil remains, on the whole, evidence against the existence of God, though hardly decisive evidence against it.

Thirdly and finally, Swinburne addresses the question of "divine hiddenness". If God exists and wants us to know and love Him, as Christians say, then why does He not make his presence better known? Surely, it would be no trouble for God to endow each and every one of His rational creatures with a firm, deep and well-grounded sense of His presence in their lives; it would also be an extremely efficient method for doing so. Yet the phenomenon of the honest agnostic, i.e. the philosopher who has studied the case for God's existence yet remains unconvinced and thus does not believe is surely an evil that God could have easily prevented. Can the evil of honest agnosticism be squared with the existence of a loving God?

Swinburne believes that it can. If the presence of God were so palpable that no one could seriously doubt that fact, our free will would once again be compromised since our awareness of divine disapproval and the likelihood of divine punishment attending our failures to do as we ought would have a tendency to corrupt our commitment to morality through the influence of self-interest and fear. Because of the need to preserve the autonomy of our moral agency, God has good reason not make His existence so evident that it cannot be denied. On the other hand, Swinburne has argued that there is enough evidence for God's existence to make God's existence more credible than not, thus enough to make His existence reasonable or rationally credible even if not inescapable. This is what we would expect, if theism were true: there is enough evidence to incline one to believe in God without making that belief rationally irresistible. In that case, however, the possibility that some might resist it on the grounds of insufficient evidence, such as the honest agnostic does, cannot be wholly excluded. Hence, far from disproving theism, the existence of the honest agnostic is, in an odd way, an additional confirmation of it. Swinburne suggests that, at least in this life, the honest agnostic is providing a good both for himself and for the religious believer and in so doing is unwittingly doing God's work!

Inference to the Best Explanation and the Future of Inductivism

Swinburne maintains that given the intrinsic or prior probability of theism, its probability given the positive evidence for theism and the unlikelihood that this evidence would obtain in a world in which theism was false that the overall probability of theism is greater than .5 even when the residual evidence against theism represented by evil is subtracted from the account. However, given that no real numerical values can be attached to the variables in the Bayes Theorem, this judgment must ultimately remain an appeal to intuition and it is not surprising that there are others, such as J. L. Mackie, whose intuition leads to a different result. While Bayesianism provides the appearance of scientific rigour and methodology in the discussion of God's existence, it is also controversial, both in its principles and its results. Not surprisingly, then, not all inductivist theists are committed to Bayesianism.

A different approach to the inductive assessment of the evidence for theism can be found in *inference to the best explanation*, a generalized version of the scientific method applied to contexts, such as the assessment of competing worldviews, in which ordinary methods of empirical confirmation and falsification are not applicable. The American "pragmaticist" C. S. Peirce was the first to attempt this sort of generalization in his account of "scientific" reasoning as constituted by three cognitive processes: *abduction* (hypothesis formation, grounded in the "surprise principle'), *deduction* (which derives testable consequences from hypotheses) and *induction* (which uses observation and experiment to test for those consequences). Peirce then applies this to the question of God's existence in his essay "A Neglected Argument for God's Existence."[1] Basil Mitchell suggests something similar in his idea of a cumulative case for God's existence, a kind of informal inductive argument that does not make claims about mathematical probability, but about reasonableness or credibility according to standards appropriate to the context in which the question is being discussed. More recently, attempts have been made to specify general criteria for what counts as a best explanation, including such standards as simplicity, coherence, scope, fecundity and efficacy. To date, however, such proposals have yet to bear significant fruit. Inductivism shows promise but still remains very much a work in progress.

---

1   See Anderson (1984) 118–84.

Chapter Four

Post-Deductivism

Nelson Pike's "Hume on Evil" can be seen to be the origin of the inductivist paradigm initiated by the atheistic response to his refutation of the deductive argument from evil. The same article can arguably be seen as the origin of what I will call the "Post-Deductivist" paradigm in the philosophy of religion as well in Pike's anticipation of that same atheistic response. To the claim that there are no plausible reasons that would justify the theistic God in permitting evil, Pike maintains that there is no reason to suppose that if there were such reasons that we would be privy to them; the mere possibility that there may be such reasons is sufficient to refute the deductive argument from evil and the theist is not obligated even to provide candidates for such reasons in order to be absolved from the charge of irrationality in embracing belief in God. This "hard-nosed" approach becomes characteristic of the Post-Deductivists, a school of largely Protestant philosophers who, like Pike, were trained in the Analytic tradition and attempt to use its methods and techniques to undermine the atheistic consensus that firmly dominated philosophy of religion in the 1950's and '60's.

In contrast to Catholicism, traditional Protestantism in the nineteenth and twentieth centuries was generally hostile to natural theology and rational apologetics. For some Protestants, the demand for rational justification was seen as derogating from the centrality of the doctrine of justification by faith alone. After all, if God's existence could be known with certainty by reason alone, what need would there be for faith? For others, such as Karl Barth and Emil Brunner, the supposition that God's existence could be rationally discussed supposes that the unregenerate sinner and the elect live in a common cognitive world, which they claim is contrary to Biblical teaching.[1] In the intellectual milieu in which the leading post-Deductivists were trained, the Protestant philosophical school known Presuppositionalism was prominent.[2] According to this school, every philosophy is embedded in and articulates a *worldview*, a global theory or way of making sense of reality that provides the foundational perspective dictating all one's substantive beliefs.[3] Since worldviews are global perspectives on reality, there is no more general perspective from which worldviews can be compared or criticised; ultimately, one's commitment to a worldview can only be an object of choice, not rational justification. Christianity is a worldview, according to this tradition, founded in the acceptance of the Bible as the word of God which dictates all of one's further substantive beliefs, including those concerning the natural and social sciences. From this perspective, there can be no rational apologetics or even common ground for discussion between Christians and non-Christians. At most, there can be a kind of negative apologetic that reveals the contradictions inherent in all non-Christian worldviews and thus shows them to fail according to their own standards of adequacy.

Although none of the Post-Deductivist analytic theists who emerged in the 1960's embraced Presuppositionalism, they evinced the generally hostile attitude of earlier Protestants to the program of natural theology and to the then-reigning Deductivist paradigm and proposed to more or less systematically dismantle its presuppositions. Although it took several decades to achieve cohesion, by the turn of the twenty-first century a fully articulated Post-Deductivist perspective had finally emerged. In this chapter I will attempt to chart its development.

---

1   For a comprehensive though perhaps overly critical summary of the views of Barth and Brunner, see Blanshard (1974),
2   For an account of Presuppositionalism see G. H. Clark's Wheaton Lectures in Nash (1968) 25–122; for a critical perspective on Presuppositionalism, see Hackett (1957) 53–78 and Sproul, Gerstner and Lindsley (1984), 183–318.
3   See Naugle (2002) *passim*, especially his discussion of Kuyper and Bavinck, 16–25.

Deductivism and the Ethics of Belief

Deductivism, as we have seen, regards deductive proof as the appropriate standard for epistemic justification in the case of God's existence. According to the analytic atheists, the case for negative atheism resides in the refutation of the traditional proofs for God's existence and the case for positive atheism rests largely on the argument from evil. However, with the failure of the deductive argument from evil, the case for positive atheism from within the deductivist perspective largely collapses. Given that neither the theist nor the atheist is able to meet the rigorous standards required by Deductivism, the contest between them seems to have been largely inconclusive and agnosticism the obvious result from the rational point of view. This leaves open the possibility, attractive to many Protestants, that one might make the "leap of faith", eschewing any concern about rational justification as irrelevant to the question of belief, perhaps on Jamesian grounds.

However, some analytic atheists were content to make do with negative atheism, maintaining that atheism, not agnosticism, is the default position in the debate over God's existence. According to Norwood Russell Hanson, Antony Flew and Michael Scriven, the position of theists and atheists in this debate is not equal.[1] Instead, since the theist makes the positive claim, he or she must carry the burden of proof in the debate over God's existence, whereas the atheist need not prove anything in order to carry the day. Thus, just as in court the presumption of innocence requires that the prosecution prove its case beyond a reasonable doubt, whereas the defence need not prove anything in order to win acquittal, so too in the debate over God's existence we must recognize the *presumption of atheism*. The failure of the theist to provide valid and sound arguments for God's existence thus entails atheism, not agnosticism and the necessity of providing such proofs is life and death for religious belief. Put simply, it is irrational to believe in God in the absence of such proofs and anyone who does so is acting in a manner contrary to one's fundamental doxastic obligations. For, as W. K. Clifford famously argued, it is wrong, always and everywhere, to believe without adequate evidence: one cannot be *epistemically* justified by faith

---

1   See Hanson (1957), Scriven (1966) and Flew (1966).

and to believe in God without adequate evidence is to be wilfully irrational.

The Post-Deductivist response to the Presumption of Atheism takes the radical course of challenging its epistemological presuppositions, which the Post-Deductivists identified as Evidentialism and Foundationalism. Evidentialism is the view that a belief is rational, hence doxastically permissible, only to the extent that it is based on evidence. On this view, theistic belief will only be doxastically permissible if it can be justified on the basis of evidence, such as that represented by the traditional proofs for God's existence. Evidentialism, in turn, generally rests on the thesis known as Foundationalism, i.e. that knowledge is possible only on the supposition that it can be rooted in epistemic foundations consisting of self-evident or incorrigible truths capable of supporting the truth of my knowledge-claims. One relevant way of formulating Foundationalism would be as follows:

> F: We ought only to believe those propositions that are either self-evident, incorrigible for me or can be apodictically deduced from propositions that are either self-evident or incorrigible for me.

According to Alvin Plantinga, the leading Post-Deductivist, this principle is highly problematic. For one thing, it is self-refuting, since it is itself neither self-evident, nor incorrigible for me, nor deducible from any self-evident or incorrigible propositions. Further, most contemporary philosophers have come to see that Foundationalism is an unworkable epistemic model, incapable of justifying most if indeed any of our knowledge-claims. To the extent that Evidentialism presupposes Foundationalism, then, it fails on the same grounds that Foundationalism does, or, at any rate, is just as controversial as the view upon which it rests. In either case, Evidentialism can hardly claim to be a universally binding principle of the ethics of belief.[1]

Of course, all of this will be beside the point if theism is demonstrably false, i.e. the burden of positive atheism can be successfully carried. However, Protestant philosophers of the 1960's and '70's generally argued that, just as theists have failed to produce any successful proofs for God's existence, athe-

---

[1] See Plantinga's "Is Belief in God Rational" in Delaney (1979) 7–27 and "Reason and Belief in God" originally published in 1983; reprinted in Sennett, 102–62.

ists have failed to show that God's existence is impossible. By the standards claimed to be applicable by deductivist analytic atheists of the 1950's, then, neither side can claim to have made out its case. Given the failure of argument for the Presumption of Atheism, the way is left open for religious belief based on faith rather than reason. However, the challenge of Inductivism still needs to be faced. The American Protestant analytic philosophers rejected the inductivist approach represented by Swinburne; Plantinga, especially, was critical of Swinburne's Bayesian approach to the justification of belief in God. They also rejected Swinburne's attempts at theodicy as fundamentally wrong-headed, taking instead the "hard-nosed" approach of Pike's "Hume on Evil", that the existence and quantity of evil in the world is arguably no evidence *at all* against God's existence. As I shall now relate, Plantinga and his followers have continued to develop this idea down through the years.

The Post-Deductivists on Evil

Nelson Pike, holding the analytic atheists' feet to the fire, maintained that it was sufficient to refute the deductive argument from evil that it be merely logically possible that God have a reason for permitting evil in the world. Pike, for his own part, expressed agnosticism about whether or not, if there were such reasons, we would be able to know what they are – as far as he was concerned, it did not matter for the purposes of refuting Mackie, McCloskey and Scriven. Plantinga, in his *God and Other Minds*, offered a couple of scenarios that he thought might serve to show what some of the possible reasons that would permit God to allow evil might be. Moral evil, he says, might be necessary for the possibility of moral agency, in which case the moral evil that exists may simply be a consequence of the misuse of free will. In a like manner, natural evil might be the product of the malevolence of powerful spiritual evil beings, such as demons or devils, exercising their own free will. Plantinga emphasizes that he is not committed to the truth of these claims – what he collectively calls the Free Will Defense – only their logical possibility. He sees no reason why we should suppose that, if God is justified in permitting evil, we should be able to know the reason for this.[1]

However, the inductivist version of the problem of evil raises a rather dif-

---
1   See Plantinga (1967) 131–35.

ferent challenge for the theist. The exponent of the evidential or probabilistic version of the problem of evil does not claim that the fact of evil provides the basis for a deductive disproof of God's existence; rather, the fact of evil is used as inductive evidence against the claim that God exists, as a ground for saying that God's existence is highly improbable or unlikely given that fact. A powerful version of this argument is due to William L. Rowe.[1] According to Rowe, there exist apparently gratuitous evils in the world, evils that are neither necessary for nor productive of any further goods. For example, consider the case of a fawn ("Bambi") caught in a forest fire and badly burned who lingers in agony for a few days before finally succumbing to exposure. A good God, says Rowe, would be both able and willing to prevent such evils from occurring. Thus, their occurrence is strong inductive evidence against the existence of God, enough evidence to make belief in God unreasonable even if not logically contradictory; it will not be enough to simply suggest that it is logically possible that God has a good reason for permitting these evils in order to save belief in God from the charge of irrationality given the evidence.

Or is it? Post-Deductivists apparently think it is. Eschewing, as I have said, the theodical approach, the Post-Deductivists have instead presented more elaborate and sophisticated defences of Pike's agnostic response to the challenge of evil. Perhaps the best known of these is that developed by Steven Wykstra.[2] According to Wykstra, evil is only *evidence* against religious belief (as opposed to a trial of faith) if it is reasonable for us to believe that, if God existed and had reasons for permitting evils such as the "Bambi" case, that we should know what they were. Suppose that I wonder whether or not I have aphids on my rose bushes. I stand at my kitchen window, squint my eyes and take a good look at my rose bushes from a distance of twenty yards. I don't see any aphids and so conclude that there are none. But this hardly counts as a reasonable belief, even if it happens to be true; there is no prospect that if I had aphids on my rose bushes I would be able to see them under those conditions. By the same token, the fact that I can't conceive of any reason why God would permit the sort of evil represented by the "Bambi" case is only evidence that there are no such reasons on the supposition that, if there were such reasons, I would be able to conceive

---

1   See Rowe (1983); reprinted in Howard-Snyder (1994) 1–11.
2 See Wykstra (1987) reprinted in Howard-Snyder (1994) 126–150.

of them. Traditional Christian piety asserts that there is no prospect of this and Rowe cannot prove otherwise. The inductive argument from evil, then, turns out to be no more successful than the deductive argument from evil.

Well, perhaps, though many atheists will see this as special pleading. In any event, this should be enough to illustrate the contention that what characterizes the Post-Deductivists is their radicalism, characterized by an intransigence that rivals that of their anti-theist opponents. This radicalism is further expressed in the thesis that belief in God may be rational even if not based on evidence at all. The positive project of Post-Deductivism consists in the attempt to show how this can be the case. I will now briefly sketch these developments.

The Parity Argument Strategy

Since the early 1970's, Protestant analytic philosophers, such as George Mavrodes, Nicholas Wolterstorff and Alvin Plantinga have been offering a two-pronged negative apologetic on behalf of religious belief. On the one hand, they have refused to play by the rules laid down by the analytic atheists, stoutly resisting the idea that theistic belief requires proof, evidence or justification in order to count as rational. On the other hand, they have explored alternate, non-Foundationalist approaches to epistemology that favour externalist over internalist accounts of epistemic justification (or *warrant*) and focus on the notion of *properly basic beliefs*, i.e. beliefs that we reasonably accept without the need for epistemic justification of either a deductive or inductive sort.

One early version of this approach has become known as the parity argument strategy. One of the first to use this strategy was George Mavrodes, who accused analytic atheism of an epistemic double standard in its evaluation of the evidence for God's existence provided by religious experience.[1] On the on hand, they treat, e.g. ordinary perceptual evidence as unproblematic in relation to everyday empirical claims; on the other, they treat religious experience as somehow aberrant or suspect as empirical evidence for the claims of religion. However, when we look at the supposed reasons why we ought to do this, we find that ordinary perceptual evidence is just as problematic as religious experience. So, for example, C. B. Martin claims that ordinary perceptual claims can

---
1   See Mavrodes (1970)

be checked or verified by further experiences, whereas religious experiences cannot.[1] In fact, however, says Mavrodes, unless we can take some perceptual experiences as veridical in and of themselves, it will be useless to try to verify some perceptual experiences by reference to others, since those perceptual experiences will be just as much in need of verification as the experiences they were invoked to justify. So, either we must just accept some perceptual experiences at fact value or embrace scepticism about perceptual experiences generally. Since it is not reasonable to embrace scepticism, it must therefore be reasonable for us to accept some perceptual experiences at face value despite the fact that such experiences cannot provide an absolute guarantee for the truth of the perceptual judgements they incline us to accept. How, then, is it unreasonable for someone to accept at least some apparently clear and distinct religious experiences at face value on the same terms and thus the religious claims they incline us to accept? Notice that Mavrodes does not argue that it *is* reasonable for us to do this, only that it is *no less* reasonable for us to do this than to accept everyday, garden-variety perceptual judgements. Mavrodes is satisfied with "epistemic parity."

Other philosophers in the Post-Deductivist camp have followed suit. In *God and Other Minds*, Plantinga develops a parallel between the traditional analogical version of the teleological argument and Descartes' analogical argument for the existence of other minds. In both cases, says Plantinga, we have a powerful intuition that when tricked out as a philosophical argument appears to have certain weaknesses. Nevertheless, we have no better reason for believing in other minds than those provided by Descartes' analogical argument and are surely reasonable in accepting the conclusion of the argument despite our awareness of the weakness of that argument. By the same token, the theist ought to be able to accept the conclusion of the teleological argument on the same terms; scepticism is no more an epistemic requirement in the latter case than in the former one.

Perhaps the most sophisticated exponent of the parity argument strategy is William P. Alston, who in a series of articles and books published in the late 1980s and early 90s developed the epistemic parallel between perceptual experience and religious experience at great length, concluding that, despite obvious differences between the two cases, religious experience (properly understood

---

1 See Martin (1965); he is no relation to Michael Martin.

and assessed) is just as reliable as perceptual experience and therefore the claim that God exists based on religious experience is just as credible as the claim that an external world exists based on perceptual experience.[1] Scepticism remains an option, of course, but the point is that, given the epistemic parity here, one is not allowed to pick and choose what one is going to be sceptical about in this context; it is arbitrary to reject religious experience as a reasonable ground for belief in God and at the same time accept sense-perception as a reasonable ground for belief in an external world. Alston has since generalized his approach, constructing a thorough-going "pluralistic" epistemological theory that he hopes will combine the best aspects of both internalist (Evidentialist) and externalist (Reliabilist) epistemologies. Plantinga has done so as well with his "Reformed Epistemology", the centrepiece of what he calls "Christian Philosophy." To this project we now turn.

Plantinga's Reformed Epistemology

Beginning in the 1960's and especially following the publication of Edmund Gettier's short paper, "Is Justified True Belief Knowledge?" the stranglehold of traditional Foundationalism began to loosen in epistemology and a number of alternatives to traditional *internalist* epistemology (i.e. epistemological theories that require that the grounds warranting belief be available in principle to the believer) began to appear. Under various titles, the new *externalist* epistemology attempted to treat knowledge as the causal product of the influence of the external world on our cognitive ("knowledge-producing") faculties. The most prominent of these externalist epistemologies was *Reliabilism*, pioneered by Alvin Goldman.[2] According to Reliabilism, our beliefs have warrant just in case they are the causal products of reliable cognitive faculties, i.e. cognitive faculties that produce a high proportion of true as opposed to false beliefs. Plantinga's project, carried out in a trilogy of books published between 1993 and 2004, is best understood in the context of this new epistemological horizon.

In *Warrant: The Current Debate* Plantinga takes the lay of the land and

---

1 See Alston (1989) and (1991).
2 See Goldman (1986) for a canonical presentation of this view.

engages in a critical examination of the major extant epistemological theories.[1] He characterizes the central problem of epistemology as that of accounting for the warrant attaching to our knowledge-claims, defining warrant as that property, whatever it is, that when added to true belief yields knowledge. He first turns to traditional internalist epistemology, criticising both Foundationalism and Coherentism (characterized by the "coherence theory of justification") as incapable of providing an adequate account of warrant. On this basis, he concludes that warrant is not constituted by any proof, evidence or justification that might be available, even in principle, to the knowing subject. He then turns to contemporary externalist epistemologies, and considers reliabilist and naturalistic epistemologies. In each case he presents a version of essentially the same argument, maintaining that, no matter how the doxastic evidential or causal conditions for warrant are specified, it is possible for all those conditions to obtain and yet for the knowing subject not to possess warrant. Most of these arguments are variations on the Gettier problem.

In *Warrant and Proper Function*, Plantinga presents his own general epistemology, one solidly grounded in the externalist tradition.[2] According to Plantinga, warrant is a the product of reliable cognitive faculties when functioning properly, i.e. in accordance with a design plan that guarantees that beliefs formed in accordance with those faculties are likely to be true, in an environment suitable for the proper functioning of those faculties. Like many radical externalists, Plantinga supposes that we do not have any control over the process of belief-formation and no way to tell whether or not our beliefs have warrant; we have no choice but simply to assume that this is case. Given the limitations of our cognitive situation, then, we simply have to take the great majority of our occurrent, spontaneously occurring beliefs, such as those produced by sense-experience, memory, anticipation of the future based on past experience, etc. as *properly basic beliefs*, i.e. beliefs that are warranted but not justified by evidence. Plantinga emphasizes that these beliefs are neither arbitrary nor groundless; they have grounds in everyday experience and have proven to be reliable in practice. Furthermore, he allows that there are well-known defeaters for our everyday belief-claims that rebut or undercut otherwise properly basic beliefs. However,

---

1   See Plantinga (1993a) *passim*.
2   See Plantinga (1993b), *passim* but especially 3–20, where his basic position is outlined.

he concludes, those properly basic beliefs for which we have no such defeaters are reasonably taken by us to be warranted, hence something that we know.

The question of whether or not belief in God is justified is essentially a matter of whether or not belief in God is a properly basic belief, i.e. one produced by a properly-functioning cognitive faculty in an environment conducive to its operation according to its design-plan, which plan is directed on the production of true beliefs. In his *Warranted Christian Belief*, Plantinga proposes that this will be the case if there is a special cognitive faculty, Calvin's *Sensus Divinitatis*, which informs every human being of this fact.[1] According to Calvin, every human being is a sinner in revolt against God, hence with every incentive to deny God's existence. At the same time, each of us has a "sense of God" within us that testifies to His existence and is sufficient to convict us for our failure to believe in Him and to do His will. What Plantinga adds to this is an account of how the testimony of this "sixth sense" can constitute knowledge for us. Since the *sensus divinitatis* is an autonomous cognitive faculty producing spontaneous beliefs, its products are candidates for properly basic belief, just like those of other autonomous cognitive faculties such as sense-perception and memory. These beliefs being warranted, then, does not depend on their being provable or justified by evidence, and it is no excuse for non-belief, as Bertrand Russell supposed it was, to say that there was not enough evidence. Basic beliefs do not recommend themselves on the basis of evidence, but simply through being spontaneously occurring beliefs that remain undefeated. Of course, there are well-known candidate defeaters for the claim that God exists, but it is sufficient to turn these aside to simply show that they fail to defeat theistic belief and for this purpose a purely negative apologetic of the "hard nosed" variety is sufficient. So then, if belief in God is an undefeated properly basic belief, then it is one that is probably warranted for us, or at any rate no less warranted than any of the other properly basic beliefs that we think it rational for us to accept. The believer, then, is perfectly within his or her rights to accept that belief despite the fact that it cannot be justified by any sort of apodictic proof or incorrigible evidence.

---

1   See Plantinga (2004) 267–353.

Plantinga and Wolterstorff: Christian Philosophy

Plantinga and his one-time colleague Nicholas Wolterstorff both attended Calvin College in Grand Rapids, Michigan. At Calvin, students were encouraged to think of Christianity as a worldview, not merely as a set of religious doctrines, and to extend the Christian worldview to encompass all of the arts and sciences in an effort to win every thought for Christ. Unlike the standard Catholic view, which regards (e.g.) philosophy and theology as autonomous disciplines, Calvin students were taught that there is a Christian perspective on or way of doing, not just philosophy, but psychology, history, economics, political science and so on. Both Plantinga and Wolterstorff have endorsed this view, as a kind of generalization of Reformed Epistemology, under the name Christian Philosophy.

In his essay "Advice to Christian Philosophers" Plantinga identifies four basic tasks that Christian philosophers might undertake, the last of which he calls the construction of a "Christian Philosophy", i.e. a philosophy explicitly founded on and expressive of the Christian worldview.[1] Such a philosophy would take the (conservative) Protestant Christian worldview as its starting point and then attempt to reconceive both the task of the philosopher and the basic problems of philosophy in Christian terms and then use Christian doctrines to seek insight into the proper solutions to these problems. The alternative, Plantinga warns, is to allow those whose worldviews are contrary to, or even hostile to, Christian religious belief to set the agenda, terms and standards for philosophical debate, thereby ruling out the possibility of a fair hearing for Christianity. His own work in epistemology can be seen as an example of this sort of project.

In Wolterstorff, Post-Deductivism meets Post-Modernism.[2] Taking it to have been shown by the course of twentieth-century philosophy, both in the analytic and continental traditions, that the idea of a neutral, philosophical or even scientific reason has been debunked, Wolterstorff maintains that not just Christian philosophers, but Christians involved in every branch of intellectual inquiry ought to be explicitly guided by their Christian commitments in designing their research, formulating hypotheses and theories and seeking confirmation for their views. While extending the same privilege to those of contrary or

---

1 Reprinted in Sennett (1998) 296–315
2 Wolterstorff (1979)

opposing worldviews and admitting that one's faith-commitment may undergo modification in response to inquiry, Wolterstorff believes that one's Christian commitment ought to provide the "control beliefs" for Christians involved in intellectual inquiry and even allow those beliefs to dictate one's political and economic commitments as well. Perhaps "intelligent design" theory in biology represents an attempt at this sort of thing; if so, we can only wait and see if (as I strongly doubt) anything worthwhile comes of it. How ever this turns out, the prospects for a Christian philosophy seem initially more hopeful, though the abandonment of the notion of neutral reason and the autonomy of philosophical inquiry may well turn out to be a double-edged sword in the hands of those who oppose religious belief.

Chapter Five

Recent Work on the Traditional Arguments for God's Existence

In the late 1960s, it was generally taken to be the case that all of the arguments for God's existence had been shown to be wanting and that, as even many theists were ready to concede, that God's existence could not be proven. One reaction to this, as we have seen, was to claim that faith, not reason, was the appropriate ground for religious belief; another was to attempt to reconceive the appropriate evidential standard for belief in God, replacing rational demonstration with inductive probability or the thesis that religious belief is properly basic. At the same time, however, distinctly new and modern versions of the traditional arguments for God's existence were being crafted as a consequence of new discoveries in logic and natural science. In this chapter I will review these results.

The Ontological Argument

Modal logic deals with the degrees or modes of truth that propositions can possess. Intuitively, some propositions are necessarily true (e.g. 2+2=4), others are necessarily false (e.g. 2+2=5) and still others are contingent, i.e. neither necessarily true nor necessarily false (e.g. "4 equals the number of my brothers."). Although interest in modal logic goes back to the time of Aristotle and the Megarians, it was not until the twentieth century that any real progress was made in the understanding of modality and modal concepts. The crucial breakthrough resulted from the work of a Nebraska high school student, Saul Kripke, in the late 1950's, known as possible worlds semantics. According to this scheme of interpretation, all of the central modal concepts could be defined by reference to the notion of a possible world, a way the world might have been construed as a *maximal* state-of-affairs, i.e. one in which every proposition has a determinate truth-value. In the 1960's, Plantinga was able to show that what Kripke had demonstrated for modality *de dicto* (i.e. regarding propositions) could be applied to modality *de re* (i.e. concerning things) as well. This made modal logic applicable to the analysis of problems in metaphysics as well, a project undertaken by Plantinga in his books *The Nature of Necessity* and *God, Freedom and Evil*.[1]

Plantinga was not the first to attempt to revive the ontological argument, however. In the 1940's, Charles Hartshorne claimed to have discovered as second, modal version of the Ontological Argument in Anselm's *Proslogion* III and over the next several decades he continued to refine and develop this argument.[2] In 1960, Norman Malcolm published his essay "Anselm's Ontological Argument" in the *Philosophical Review* in which he defended a version of the same argument that Hartshorne had pioneered.[3] This version of the argument attempts to show that if God's existence is even so much as possible, then God actually exists. The argument can be summarized as follows:

1. If God does not exist, then His existence is logically impossible.
2. If God exists, then His existence is logically necessary.
3. God's existence is either logically impossible or it is logically necessary.
4. If God's existence is logically impossible, then the concept of God is self-contradictory.
5. The concept of God is not self-contradictory.
6. Therefore, God's existence is logically necessary.
7. Therefore, God exists.

This argument created quite a stir when it first appeared and attracted quite a bit of criticism, most notably from Plantinga himself. Nevertheless, within a few years Plantinga was prepared to endorse his own, possible-worlds version of the above argument, which can be summarized as follows:

---

1 See Plantinga (1974a) and (1974b).
2 See Hartshorne (1940) and (1965).
3 Reprinted in Plantinga (1965), 136–59.

1. God=df a maximally great being, i.e. one that exemplifies maximal excellence in every possible world.
2. Maximal greatness is possibly exemplified.
3. If so, then God exists in some possible world.
4. God cannot exist in some possible world without existing in every possible world.
6. So, if God exists in any possible world, then God exists in every possible world.
7. So, God exists in every world.
8. The actual world is a possible world.
9. Therefore, God exists in the actual world, which is to say
10. God exists.

Plantinga defines maximal excellence as the possession of omnipotence, omniscience, omnibenevolence and necessary existence. A maximally great being will possess these properties essentially, i.e. as inseparable from its being in the same way that "having three sides" is inseparable from triangularity, and thus possess these properties in every possible world. As such, if God exists in any possible world whatsoever, then God must exist in every world. But, since maximal greatness is possibly exemplified by the usual standards (e.g. it is not obviously self-contradictory), then God does exist in all possible worlds. Since the actual world is a possible world (i.e. one way that the world might be) then God exists in the actual world as well, from which it follows that God actually exists.

Plantinga stops short of claiming that the revived ontological argument is a proof for God's existence, since at least one of the premises of the argument, i.e. that maximal greatness is possibly exemplified, remains unproven and may well be incapable of proof. Nevertheless, the argument is vindicated insofar as it is a demonstrably valid deductive argument that depends only on a very minimal assumption that many atheists are willing to concede without argument; other valid versions of the argument have also been constructed in recent years. Although some critics continue to resist this argument, it remains a major achievement of recent analytic philosophy of religion.

The Cosmological Argument

Although analytic philosophers of the 1950's and '60's concentrated largely on the Five Ways, in the 1970's philosophers began to discover and investigate different versions of the cosmological argument, in particular those developed in the early eighteenth century by Clarke and Leibniz, which were perceived to be stronger (or at least more sophisticated) than those of Aquinas. William L. Rowe states the argument in a simplified way as follows:

1. Every being that exists is either a self-existent being or a dependent being.
2. Not every being could be a dependent being.
3. Therefore, there exists a self-existent being.[1]

The argument for the first premise goes as follows:

1a. Whatever exists has a cause for its existence.
1b. That cause is either intrinsic to that being or extrinsic to it.
1c. Therefore, every being that exists is either a self-existent being or a dependent being.

The argument for the second premise goes as follows:

2a. The existence of any dependent being has to be explained by reference to the operation of some further being.
2b. Even the postulation of a temporally infinite series of such beings would not explain why any such beings exist at all.
2c. Therefore, not every being could be a dependent being.

From this the conclusion, that a self-existent being exists, can be validly derived. Premise 1a is a version of the principle of sufficient reason (PSR) to which both Leibniz and Clarke appeal. Both regard this principle to be a self-evident truth and use it to exclude the possibilities that anything could be produced spontaneously from nothing or by mere chance. Premise 1b envisages the possibility that there is at least one being that possesses its existence intrinsically rather than having received it from something else. Such a being would possess the cause, reason or explanation of its existence from within its own being, perhaps as a consequence of its unique nature or essence. Although it is difficult to conceive how this could be case, we cannot simply exclude the possibility of such a being on that ground alone and, given the PSR, we would be rationally justified in positing such a being without full understanding of how its existence could be self-explanatory, just as we do with many theoretical posits in contemporary physics. Rowe, for example, offers an analogy drawn from Anselm to illustrate the rationality of this practice: we find things in the world that are *derivatively*

---

1   See Rowe (2007) 19–32; for a more extended presentation of the argument, see Rowe (1998) 60–167.

hot, i.e. hot but not the source of the heat they contain. Since these things are hot yet not as a consequence of their own natures or operations, we naturally suppose that they derive their heat from some other source. However, it is useless to suppose that the heat is derived in every case from some other thing that is hot without being the source of its own heat, since in that case we have no explanation for where the heat being transferred came from in the first place. We therefore naturally infer to the existence of something, e.g. the element of fire, which is non-derivatively hot, i.e. intrinsically hot or hot by nature, to explain the heat of derivatively hot things; this will hold regardless of we have any ready explanation for the intrinsic hotness of fire.

With regard to the argument for premise 2, it is sub-premise 2b that has attracted the lion's share of criticism. According to Hume and Paul Edwards, it is sufficient to explain the existence of any series of dependent beings that each of the members of the series is explained by reference to other members of the series; if we postulate that the series is beginningless and thus consists of an infinite number of temporally ordered members, we avoid the difficulty of having to account for the existence of the series as a whole.[1] Rowe, for one, disagrees with this: the question "Why does this series exist at all?" is not answered by an explanation of the existence of each of the members of the series in terms of other members of the series. It seems conceivable that the series need not have existed at all; as such, neither need any of its members have existed. As such, we cannot account for the existence of the series as a whole (as opposed to its non-existence) simply by reference to that of its members. Since this series is not plausibly thought to be a self-existent being, we have ample reason, given the PSR, to posit a distinct, self-existent being as the external cause of that series.[2]

While Rowe maintains that the Clarke/Leibniz cosmological argument is valid and escapes the standard criticisms levelled against it, he does not endorse the argument. In fact, Rowe is an atheistic philosopher of religion who identifies the problem of the argument with its reliance on the PSR. Not every philosopher, Rowe points out, accepts the PSR and the principle cannot be proven to be true. Of course, if the principle is self-evident, there is no prospect of any such proof, so the demand for it can hardly be legitimate. Nevertheless, the

---

1   See Edwards (1959) and references.
2   See Rowe (1998) 144–67.

principle remains controversial and may even be false. Nevertheless, despite its shortcomings Rowe concludes that the cosmological argument is still viable for philosophical discussion.

The cosmological argument receives a much needed "shot in the arm" from modern "Big Bang" cosmology which, while first proposed in the 1920's, did not finally become universally accepted by scientists until the mid-1960's. According to "Big Bang" theory, the universe is not infinitely old but in fact of finite age, the product of an initial explosion resulting from the unstable character of the initial state of the universe, known as the "singularity." The likely truth of this empirical fact undermines those objections to the cosmological argument that depend on the possibility of such a series; it also lends strong empirical support to a traditional version of the cosmological argument, a staple of medieval Jewish and Muslim theology, known as the *Kalam* cosmological argument, which can be simply stated as follows:

1. Whatever begins to exist has a cause for its existence.
2. The physical universe began to exist.
3. Therefore, the physical universe has a cause for its existence.

This cause, it is urged, cannot be anything physical since nothing physical existed prior to the existence of the universe; the cause of the universe, then, must be a non-physical being, i.e. God.[1]

There have numerous attempts to evade the clutches of this argument through the postulation of some sort of universe-generating mechanism that existed prior to the "big bang" or through appeal to the "Anthropic Principle" which claims that the fact that we exist in some way explains the existence of the universe. There is no room here to discuss these proposals; I will simply note in passing that none of them has been shown to have any traction beyond the level of a mere speculation. Even so, this version of the cosmological argument proves to be no less dependent than the Leibniz/Clarke version on the PSR. If someone wants to insist that the universe simply "popped into existence" from nothing for

---

[1] See Craig (1979). Craig's argument has generated a large literature and he has actively defended the argument in the face of stiff criticism. However, the overall consensus, even among theistic philosophers, is that his argument is unsuccessful.

no reason in order to avoid positing God as the cause of the universe, it does not appear that he can be directly refuted. Nevertheless, it once again appears that, on very minimal assumptions that most atheists would be likely to find antecedently reasonable, there is a compelling argument for God's existence even if it falls short of being an apodictic proof.

The Teleological Argument

The teleological argument proposes to prove the existence of God from the apparent order, design and purposiveness we observe in the natural world. This argument was the most popular argument for God's existence during the seventeenth and eighteenth centuries, when natural science was growing by leaps and bounds; even the substantial critique of the argument offered by David Hume failed to do much to check its progress. However, the theory of evolution formulated by Darwin in the mid-nineteenth century dealt what many believed was a fatal blow to the argument by showing how a combination of chance and necessity could lead to the appearance of order and purposive design, at least with regard to biological adaptation. This is an impression that many people retain to this day, but it need not be correct. Throughout the twentieth century, exponents of the argument have made significant progress in rehabilitating it.

F. R. Tennant's *Philosophical Theology* appeared in 1930, long after the time that near universal consensus on the truth of evolution as a fact of the natural history of life on earth had been established.[1] Tennant nevertheless presents a surprisingly complex and sophisticated defence of the argument by pointing to more general, apparently non-random features of the universe that seem to be presupposed by the process of evolution itself. It was indeed Tennant who was the first to use the term "anthropic" of the universe as a whole: the universe, he says, is as though designed to produce self-conscious rational moral agents such as ourselves. Now this is either mere appearance or it has some foundation in reality itself and it is not credible, on the face of it, that this is a mere appearance. At the same time, this anthropic quality evident from our experience of the universe does not appear to be intrinsic to it either. So then, the most natural supposition is that this anthropic character of reality is the result of some non-

---

1 See Tennant (1930), Volume II *passim*.

natural power that has "front-loaded" the universe in such a way as to secure its anthropic character. But, of course, this naturally suggests the existence of God to play the role of the intelligent designer of the universe.

This sort of argument, evident also in Swinburne's discussion, has recently been strengthened in an intriguing way by some discoveries in modern physics. According to Barrow and Tipler, the necessary pre-conditions for intelligent life in our universe require that the values for the fundamental constants in its most primitive laws fall into an extremely narrow range.[1] Due to the fact that each of these constants is causally independent of the others, the likelihood that each of these constants should be set at precisely the point necessary in order to make intelligent life possible is extremely low – something like 10 to the 40th power. That chance could produce such an outcome seems highly improbable. On the other hand, if the universe were the product of an intelligent designer who created it specifically to insure the possibility of this result, that these constants should have the values they do would not only be explicable but to be expected. Once again, the world is as we would expect it to be if there was a God.

This argument from the "fine tuning" of the universe, if empirically sound, does appear to provide a new platform for the teleological argument, one not vulnerable to the theory of evolution. Opponents of the argument have suggested that alternative cosmological models – such as the "many worlds" hypothesis or the "oscillating universe" hypothesis might overcome the apparent long odds against chance producing a universe like this one. However, there are serious conceptual problems afflicting these hypotheses and little prospect of there being any empirical confirmation of their truth; for whatever reason, they are little regarded today.

The teleological argument looks stronger now than at any time in the last century and a half, but remains vulnerable to changes in scientific paradigm. As such, theists can never rest content with any particular version of the argument. However, as each new scientific paradigm appears, it seems to provide the foundation for a new version of the argument. So long as there are any surd facts or mechanisms presupposed but not explained by scientific theory, the

---

1 See Barrow and Tipler (1974); neither Barrow nor Tipler was a theist at this time and both resist the idea that the facts of "fine tuning" can be used to mount a teleological argument for God's existence.

existence of God will always naturally suggest itself as the final stopping point of human intellectual inquiry.

Bibliography

Alston, William P. (1989a) *Divine Nature and Human Language*, Ithaca, NY, Cornell University Press

—— (1991) *Perceiving God*, Ithaca, NY, Cornell University Press

Anderson, Douglas R. (1995) *Strands of System*, West Lafayette, IN, Purdue University Press

Ayer, A. J. (1946) *Language, Truth and Logic*, London, V. Gollancz

Barrow, John and Frank Tipler (1986) *The Anthropic Cosmological Principle*, New York, Oxford

Blanshard, Brand (1968) *Reason and Analysis*, Chicago, IL, Open Court

—— (1974) *Reason and Belief*, London, Allen and Unwin

Braithwaite, Richard (1955) *An Empiricists view of the Nature of Religious Belief*, Cambridge, England, Cambridge University Press

Burrill, Donald (1967) *The Cosmological Argument*, Garden City, NY, Anchor Books

Clifford, W. K. (1999) *The Ethics of Belief and Other Essays*, Amherst, NY, Prometheus Books

Copan, Paul and William Lane Craig (2004) *Creation Out of Nothing*, Grand Rapids, MI Baker Academic

Copan, Paul and Paul K. Moser (2003) *The Rationality of Theism*, London, Routlege

Craig, William Lane (1979) *The Kalam Cosmological Argument*, Eugene, OR, Wipf and Stock

Cupitt, Don (2001) *Taking Leave of God*, London, SCM Press

Darwin, Charles (1995) *The Origin of Species*, London, Gramercy

Davis, Stephen T., (1997) *God, Reason and Theistic Proofs*, Grand Rapids, MI, Wm. B. Eerdmans

Delaney, Cornelius (1979) *Rationality and Religious Belief*, Notre Dame, IN, Notre Dame University Press

Denzinger, Henry (1954) *Sources of Catholic Dogma*, (31st Edition, ed. Karl Rahner) Fitzwilliam, NH, Loreto Publications

Dupuis, Jacques and J. Neuner, S. J. (2001) *The Christian Faith*, New York, Alba House

Flew, Antony and Alasdair Macintyre (1955) *New Essays in Philosophical Theology*, London, SCM Publishing

Flew, Antony (1966) *God and Philosophy*, London, Hutchinson

—— (1976) *The Presumption of Atheism and Other Essays*, New York, Barnes and Noble

Gale, Richard (1991) *On the Existence and Nature of God*, New York, Cambridge University Press

Garrigou–Lagrange, Reginald (1934) *God: His Existence and His Nature*. 2 volumes, St. Louis, MO, B. Herder Book Co.

Geisler, Norman (1979) *Philosophy of Religion*, Grand Rapids, MI, Zondervan

Goldman, Alvin (1986) *Epistemology and Cognition*, Cambridge, MA, Harvard University Press

Hackett, Stuart (1957) *The Resurrection of Theism*, Grand Rapids, MI, Baker Book House

Hartshorne, Charles (1941) *Man's Vision of God*, Chicago, Willett, Clark and Company

—— (1962) *The Logic of Perfection*, LaSalle, IL, Open Court Publishing Company

—— (1965) *Anselm's Discovery*, LaSalle, IL, Open Court Publishing Company

Hepburn, Ronald (1958) *Christianity and Paradox*, London, Watts

Hick, John (1957) *Faith and Knowledge*, Ithaca, NY, Cornell University Press

—— (1970) *Evil and the God of Love*, London, Collins

Hook, Sidney (1961b) *Religious Experience and Truth*, New York, NYU Press

Howard–Snyder, Daniel (1996) *The Evidential Argument from Evil*, Bloomington, IN, University of Indiana Press

Hudson, Deal and Dennis Moran (1992), *The Future of Thomism*, Notre Dame, IN, Notre Dame University Press

Hume, David (1980) *A Treatise of Human Nature*, Oxford, Clarendon Press

—— (1984) *Dialogues Concerning Natural Religion*, Indianapolis, IN, Hackett

James, William (1979) *The Will to Believe and Other Essays*, Cambridge, MA, Harvard University Press

Joyce, G. H. (1922) *Principles of Natural Theology*, London, Longmans, Green and Company

Kant, Immanuel (1934), *Critique of Pure Reason*, London, J. M. Dent and Sons

Kenny, Anthony (1969) *The Five Ways*, New York, Shocken Books

Leslie, John (1979) *Value and Existence*, Oxford, Blackwell

Leo XIII (1879), *Aeterni Patris*, Rome, Acta Apostolica Sedis, 97ff.

Long, Eugene T. (2000) *Twentieth Century Western Philosophy of Religion*, Boston, MA, Kluwer Academic Publishers

Mackie, J. L. (1982) *The Miracle of Theism*, Oxford, Clarendon Press

Martin, C. B. (1959) *Religious Belief*, Ithaca, NY, Cornell University Press

Martin, Michael (1990) *Atheism: A Philosophical Defense*, Philadelphia, PA, Temple University Press

Martin, Michael and Ricki Monnier (2003) *The Impossibility of God*, Amherst, NY, Prometheus Books

Mavrodes, George (1970) *Belief in God*, New York, Random House

McInerny, Ralph (1961) *The Logic of Analogy*, The Hague, Martinus Nijhoff

—— (1968) *Studies in Analogy*, The Hague, Martinus Nijhoff

—— (1999) *Aquinas and Analogy*, Washington, D.C., Catholic University of America Press

Mitchell, Basil (1973) *The Justification of Religious Belief*, London, Macmillan

Morris, Thomas V. (1989) *Anselmian Explanations*, Notre Dame, IN, Notre Dame University Press

—— (1991) *Our Idea of God*, Notre Dame, IN, Notre Dame University Press

Nielsen, Kai (1971) *Contemporary Critiques of Religion*, New York, Herder and Herder

—— (1983) *An Introduction to the Philosophy of Religion*, London, Macmillan

Naugle, David K. (2002) *Worldview: History of a Concept*, Grand Rapids, MI, Wm. B. Eerdmans

Owen, H. P. (1971) *Concepts of Deity*, London, Macmillan

Owens, Joseph (1980) *St. Thomas Aquinas on the Existence of God*, Albany, NY, SUNY Press

Nash, Ronald H. (1968) *The Philosophy of Gordon H. Clark*, Philadelphia, PA, Presbyterian and Reformed Publishing Company

Pap, Arthur and Paul Edwards (1973) *A Modern Introduction to Philosophy*, NY, The Free Press

Parsons, Keith (1990) *God and the Burden of Proof*, Amherst, NY, Prometheus Books

Phillips, D. Z. (1967) *Religion and Understanding*, Oxford, Blackwell

—— (1976) *Religion without Explanation*, Oxford, Blackwell

Phillips, R. P. (1941) *Modern Thomistic Philosophy*, London, Washbourne and Oates

Pike, Nelson (1965) *God and Evil*, Englewood Cliffs, NJ, Prentice–Hall

Plantinga, Alvin (1965) *The Ontological Argument*, Garden City, NY, Anchor Books

—— (1967) *God and Other Minds*, Ithaca, NY, Cornell University Press

—— (1974) *The Nature of Necessity*, Oxford, Clarendon Press

—— (1975) *God, Freedom and Evil*, London, Allen and Unwin

—— (1993a) *Warrant: The Current Debate*, New York, Oxford University Press

—— (1993b) *Warrant and Proper Function*, New York, Oxford University Press

—— (2004) *Warranted Christian Belief*, New York, Oxford University Press

Plantinga, Alvin and Nicholas Wolterstorff (1979), *Faith and Rationality*, Notre Dame, IN, Notre Dame University Press

Pseudo–Dionysius (1987) *The Complete Works*, New York, Paulist Press

Ramsey, Ian T. (1957) *Religious Language*, London, SCM Press

—— (1964) *Models and Mystery*, London, Oxford University Press

Ross, James F. (1969) *Philosophical Theology*, Indianapolis, IN, Bobbs–Merrill

—— (1981) *Portraying Analogy*, New York, Cambridge University Press

Rowe, William (1975) *The Cosmological Argument*, Princeton, NJ, Princeton University Press

Russell, Bertrand (1957) *Why I am not a Christian*, New York, Simon and Schuster

Scriven, Michael (1966) *Primary Philosophy*, New York, McGraw–Hill

Sell, Alan P. F. (1988) *Philosophy of Religion 1875–1980*, London, Croom Helm

Sennett, James F. (1998) *The Analytic Theist*, Grand Rapids, MI, Wm. B. Eerdmans

Smart, Ninian (1969) *Philosophers and Religious Truth*, London, SCM Press

Sobel, Jordan Howard (2004) *Logic and Theism*, New York, Cambridge University Press

Sproul, R. C., John Gerstner and Arthur Lindsley (1984), *Classical Apologetics*, Grand Rapids, MI, Zondervan

Swinburne, Richard (2004) *The Existence of God* (second edition), Oxford, Clarendon Press

Tennant, F. R. (1930) *Philosophical Theology*, Cambridge, Cambridge University Press

Thomas Aquinas, St. (1964), *Summa Theologiae*, Cambridge, Blackfriars

Urmson, J. O. (1956) *Philosophical Analysis*, Oxford, Clarendon Press

Van Inwagen, Peter (1995) *God, Freedom and Mystery*, Ithaca, NY, Cornell University Press

—— (2006) *The Problem of Evil*, Oxford, Clarendon Press.

Wisdom, John (1963) *Philosophy and Psychoanalysis*, Oxford, Basil Blackwell

Wolterstorff, Nicholas (1984) *Reason within the Limits of Religion*, Grand Rapids, MI, Wm. B. Eerdmans

Yandell, Keith (1984) *Christianity and Philosophy*, Grand Rapids, MI, Wm. B. Eerdmans

Also available from www.humanities-ebooks.co.uk

Humanities Insights

General Titles
An Inroduction to Feminist Theory
An Introduction to Critical Theory
An Introduction to Rhetorical Terms

Genre FictionSightlines
Octavia E Butler: *Xenogenesis / Lilith's Brood*
Reginal Hill: *On Beulah's Height*
Ian McDonald: *Chaga / Evolution's Store*
Walter Mosley: *Devil in a Blue Dress*
Tamora Pierce: *The Immortals*

History Insights
Oliver Cromwell
The British Empire: Pomp, Power and Postcolonialism
The Holocaust: Events, Motives, Legacy *
Lenin's Revolution
Methodism and Society
The Risorgimento

Literature Insights
Conrad: *The Secret Agent*
Eliot, T S: 'The Love Song of J Alfred Prufrock' and *The Waste Land*
English Renaissance Drama: Theatre and Theatres in Shakespeare's Time *
Faulkner: *The Sound and the Fury*
Gaskell, *Mary Barton*
Hardy: *Tess of the Durbervilles*
Ibsen: *The Doll's House*
Hopkins: Selected Poems
Ted Hughes: *New Selected Poems* *
Lawrence: *Sons and Lovers*
Lawrence: *Women in Love*
Paul Scott: *The Raj Quartet*

Shakespeare titles: *Hamlet, Henry IV, The Merchant of Venice, Richard II, Richard III, The Tempest, Troilus and Cressida*
Shelley: *Frankenstein* *
Wordsworth: *Lyrical Ballads* *
Fields of Agony: English Poetry and the First World War

Philosophy Insights

American Pragmatism
Barthes
Contemporary Epistemology
Critical Thinking and Informal Logic
Ethics
Existentialism
Formal Logic
Metaethics Examined *
Modern Feminist Theory
Philosophy of Sport
Plato
Wittgenstein

Full Length Books

Sibylle Baumbach, *Shakespeare and the Art of Physiognomy* *
John Beer, *The Achievement of E M Forster*
John Beer, *Coleridge the Visionary*
Jared Curtis, ed., *The Fenwick Notes of William Wordsworth* *
Steven M. Duncan, *Analytic Philosophy of Religion: Its History since 1955*
Richard Gravil, *Master Narratives: Tellers and Telling in the English Novel*
Richard Gravil and Molly Lefebure, *The Coleridge Connection: Essays for Thomas McFarland*
John K. Hale, *Milton as Multilingual: Selected Essays 1982–2004*
John Lennard, *Of Modern Dragons and other essays on Genre Fiction* *
Colin Nicholson, *Fivefathers: Interviews with late Twentieth-Century Scottish Poets*
W J B Owen, *Understanding 'The Prelude'*
Keith Sagar, *D. H. Lawrence: Poet* *
William Wordsworth, *The Prose Works of William Wordsworth*, Volume 1 *
William Wordsworth, *The Convention of Cintra*
The Poems of William Wordsworth: Collected Reading Texts from the Cornell Wordsworth *
The Cornell Wordsworth: A Supplement *

* print versions available

www.ingramcontent.com/pod-product-compliance
Lightning Source LLC
Chambersburg PA
CBHW081500040426
42446CB00016B/3335